Surviving Motherhood

by

Donna Lagorio Montgomery

St.Johns
PUBLISHING COMPANY

Published by

St. John's Publishing, Inc,
6824 Oaklawn Avenue
Edina, MN 55435

ISBN:0-938577-00-X

Printed in the United States of America by:

Apollo Books, Inc.
107 Lafayette Street
Winona, MN 55987

First Printing: 1986

Cover design: Tim Montgomery

Dedication

To my mother and father, Leonora and John Lagorio, who were good parents.

To Karen,
Happy surviving and happy motherhood

Donna Montgomery

Acknowledgements

I gratefully acknowledge the editing contribution of my husband, Don, and the illustrations of our son, Tim. Thanks also to our eight children who gave me the experience I needed to write a book about motherhood.

PREFACE

This book presents a practical view of motherhood. You discover through one mother's experiences that your own problems are probably universal to most moms.

The sense of sisterhood in this book, plus its sense of humor, are not only helpful for mothers, but essential. You also find out how a mother survives peer groups and peer pressure. True to life "incidents" that test a mother's sanity as well as her sense of humor are revealed.

A section on children's "loves" and "hates" gives mothers a new outlook. Included here are letters to moms written by children. These letters give parents ideas about their own children's "loves," "hates," creativity, and loving thoughts.

Surviving Motherhood is a unique book that looks at family relationships. It's not meant to be all humorous, all serious, all knowing, or all correct. Rather, it's meant to be friendly, loving, and understanding. The whole idea of the book is to give mothers encouragement and practical support.

CONTENTS

IV. Children's Views

V. Grade School Mothering

VI. Mothering Teens

VII. Emotions And Mothering

VIII. Mothering Mothers

ix

I. Happiness Is Mothering

1.

Harried Mother, Enjoy Your Space

When families are young and growing, mothers tend to become a bit numbed by the burdens of child rearing. It seems there's only enough time for caretaking, and even that becomes difficult when trying to balance both a business career and family.

In earlier years, moms used to have their hands in the toilet a good part of each day, rinsing out diapers. When done with that, washing and folding them. Today disposable diapers are in, but one thing hasn't changed. Moms still see more bare bottoms, and have to clean more of them than they ever dreamed they would.

Those same kids, older now and so cool in their teenage years, would die of embarrassment if mom saw them naked. It's necessary occasionally to remind them that mom saw those rear ends enough in their infancy to last her a lifetime!

In a child's early years, mothers usually lead more limited social lives. In fact, quite frankly, there may not be any social life at all.

Even if moms could get away, many can't afford to go anywhere. Just to take a walk alone to give them breathing room is seldom possible, because most moms can't afford a babysitter. With only one household income, there's rarely enough money for extras. If both husband and wife work, there may be a little more money, but then lack of time is still a problem. Sometimes close family friends and relatives say they'll babysit with the kids to give mom a break. Unfortunately, they rarely do what they say, and mothers are reluctant to remind them.

Moms who aren't employed outside the home are told, "There's a whole world out there!" What most home-bound moms realize that others don't, is that there's also a whole world *inside* that house. It's a world to be enjoyed and relished while they're privileged to pass through it.

Sooner or later all moms get harried, many are broke, and many more get sick of those dirty diapers. As trying as such a life may become, it's only a temporary phase of motherhood. So why not enjoy it? The good memories of those dear little children should be treasured in mother's heart to help her through the years to come. Children, too, will have:

HAPPY MEMORIES

Of days spent with mom playing in the yard or at the park,
Going on walks,
Playing in the sandbox or in a playhouse,
Learning to ride a bike,
Ice skating,
Roller skating,
Walking to the ice cream store,
Watching the greening of trees in the Spring as they bud,
Picking apples in the Fall,
Baking together,
Walking around the lake,

Working together,
Shopping,
Coloring together,
Reading before bed at night.

Many things mothers do with their children seem like nothing at the time, but they mean everything later. It's important for moms to realize, therefore, that in spite of their inexperience, their child's early years can still be fun, if a mother has the good, practical, common sense to enjoy them.

2.

Mothers Need Encouragement

Since Mother's Day always falls on Sunday, everyone has more time. For example, many mothers begin that day with a treat of breakfast in bed prepared by the family. When my children were young, the breakfast was as delightful as they were able to make it. Now that they're older, breakfast in bed has become so elaborate and so big, it has to be moved downstairs to the dining room table and expanded to include the whole family. Fresh fruit, croissants, eggs, meat, cheese, special teas, Catawba juice and many other exotic treats stimulate the taste buds, while flowers grace the table and delight the eyes. Homemade Mother's Day cards announce each child's special love, and homemade or store-bought gifts are excitedly given to Mom.

The only disappointments of the day seem to have come at church. Over the years, we have moved around the country and have attended many different churches. Still, disappointment has come with every church. *No clergyman has ever given a sermon about mothers on Mother's Day* . Maybe it's just a phenomenon that's peculiar to the particular kind of churches we've been attending.

The last few years the clergyman has at least said, "Happy Mother's Day." One year recently, a mother spoke. But thinking back over the more than twenty-five years of my motherhood, Mother's Day was often designated as a "Mission Sunday" at the churches we attended. The homilists dwelt on getting contributions for some needy missions in Africa, Asia, or elsewhere. There are fifty-one other Sundays of the year to talk about the poor, but the homilists seem to have always felt the need to use Mother's Day to fulfill their mission obligation.

One year it seemed we were about to have our wish fulfilled. The homilist said he was going to talk about Mother's Day, then spent the next half-hour honoring the single woman. The one year in twenty-five when it looked like we were going to get a real Mother's Day sermon, the homilist gave a long talk about the virtues of the "much-neglected single woman." Why not talk about that on one of those fifty-one other Sundays that aren't Mother's Day?

Is our society afraid to give mothers a little support and respect on the one day set aside for them out of the whole year? There have been countless homilies about fathers on Father's Day. Why are mothers neglected? No mother expects to be gushed over. However, motherhood is very difficult. Many mothers are discouraged. Some even give up. A little pep talk is needed in churches on Mother's Day to cheer up mothers and encourage them.

If a mother finds it necessary to get a paying job outside the home in addition to doing her non-paying job in the home, she's forced to juggle two very important careers. Fathers are seldom asked to do as much as mothers. Even mothers who aren't employed outside the home full-time, are usually juggling lots of volunteer PTA, church, and community work on behalf of their own children, and children of mothers employed outside the home. It's not easy to be a mother these days, and it's extremely difficult to be a good one.

Mothers need more support than ever. They have to cope with bad TV programming, drug abuse, alcoholism, peer group pressures, high prices, shrinking income, insensitive husbands, loose society morals, and countless other adverse, out-of-control influences. Support for mothers can come in the form of advice, encouragement, reminiscences, or other kinds of help. Mothers aren't particular.

Mothers need to be recognized; not ignored. One Sunday a year isn't too much recognition for them. Tell it from the heart in whatever way is honest. Did a homilist have a difficult childhood? Tell about it. Did he or she have a happy childhood? Tell about it. Any fond memories of mother? Tell about them. Observations? Tell about them. Survival advice for mothers? Tell about it.

Mothers are tough. They've been through the fire. They've lived through kids loving them and hating them, good times and hard times. Mothers know both pride and humility, acceptance and rejection. No other group in the world is so forgiving, or has been asked to forgive so much, over and over.

Mothers have mothers of their own, and now, as mothers themselves, possess a unique perspective. Tell them almost anything, they won't be shocked. Reject them and they'll come back. The worst thing would be to ignore them. Mothers, as much as anyone, need encouragement.

3.

Appreciating Life

Where do parents begin their thoughts about life? If they have a reverence for life, do they include all life? Such questions are important, since parents influence children's attitudes. These questions don't have anything to do with organized religion. They have to do simply, but very importantly, with life itself from its lowest to its highest forms.

If you were the kind of kid who went out of your way to avoid stepping on an ant or releasing a fly outside the house instead of killing it, you understand what life is all about. You appreciate the importance of saving the Snail Darter, or other nearly-extinct species.

A life-lover rejoices in the Spring of the year, and becomes nostalgic in the Fall. A life-lover enjoys a flower while it's in the garden, and will bring plants inside the house to keep them living, rather than fill vases with cut flowers. A life-lover sees God's love

9

and purpose in all creatures. A life-lover could never consciously interfere with the process of life, because a life-lover is a serious thinker and a person with heart.

Have you ever stopped to think what happens when something interferes with life? What if Abraham Lincoln's parents had lost Abe early in life? What if his great, great, great grandparents had never been born? Go back generations in your own family. What if a distant relative had lost or ended a life? Ours isn't the only life to be considered; whole *generations* are destroyed. One life lost prematurely causes the whole world to change.

Walking through a protected nature area or wildlife refuge gives one plenty of food for thought. Have you ever noticed how some of these areas are never altered or the dead things removed? Trees die, but when they fall over, no one picks them up or clears them out. They stay where they fall, and new life begins in them and around them. New shelters are formed for birds and animals to nest in, and bugs live in them and become food for birds, as life begins anew through death. Conservationists don't tamper with the life-forms of nature, because they know nature has its own checks and balances.

Where do human beings fit into all the checks and balances? Each one of us needs to get more serious about life. We need time when we're young to observe it, study it, be awed by it. Human beings are the most blessed of creatures. We're endowed with brains to learn and think and do. Yet, of all creatures, when it comes to being responsible for our actions, we've probably done the worst job. Our free will is tempered by conscience, but we often use the one and ignore the other. Our children can't be expected to respect life if we as parents don't take the time to teach them.

Parents need to get off the merry-go-round. We're missing life. Our children grow up before we know it, while we're sitting at meetings and doing things with no lasting value. Let's take time now to slow down, love our children, and recommit our lives to celebrating creation and all life.

4.

Smelling The Roses

We're missing many good things in life. It's time we slow down and savor the beauty of our surroundings. It's time to smell the roses. We're in the middle of a most exciting universe. We should take time to carefully observe it, so we can teach our children to be good observers, too.

Day after day, month after month, year after year, nature's seasons unfold their splendors before us, but we seem to miss the beauty of their comings and goings.

The order and consistency in nature should never cease to amaze us. Even the tiniest flower on the tiniest weed is consistent year after year. A particular kind of flower has the same number of petals; leaves of the same species are always shaped the same. A snowflake has a consistent number of identical sides. Robins come back in the Spring. Buds appear on the same trees at the same time each year.

Tiny seeds become big flowers, or vegetables, or trees. The sun rises every morning in the east and sets every evening in the west. Nature's consistency is truly remarkable.

Colors in nature are consistent and true—a red tulip, a yellow buttercup, a gold and maroon marigold, a blue morning glory, a white rose, a purple iris. And every flower will be consistent in size, shape, petals, smell, and coloring. A purple eggplant, a green bean, an orange melon, yellow corn, green lettuce, yellow squash, and red tomatoes are sights to behold. Also, the smell of each will be consistent. We can even smell rain in the air, grass freshly cut, lilacs in bloom, a field of alfalfa.

We can make whistles out of grass, weave wreaths for the hair from dandelions and clover, pick bouquets for our homes, or grow food for our tables.

Lying on the ground on our back in the summer, we can smell the grass as it's growing. We can also see another world we usually don't look at, the never-ending sky. How impressive it is to observe cloud movements and see clouds form different shapes as they pass overhead. Sometimes, we even get the treat of seeing one layer of clouds go east while a higher layer goes west. Or, the reverse might happen. At night we can be overwhelmed by billions of stars, their degrees of brightness, and the many interesting patterns they seem to form.

How many of us help our children appreciate nature's wonders? Isn't it amazing that with billions of cells in our bodies, they all end up in the right place at birth? Isn't it a wonder that cats have hair, cows have leather hides, turtles have shells, fish have scales, rabbits have long ears, elephants have long trunks, giraffes have long necks, animals have instincts and we have minds? Think of it! Think of everything you can see in nature and be awed by it. Then teach your children to be awed by it.

How much must we be loved by our Creator, who shares nature with us! We and our children are never alone. We need never despair. What fun it is to smell the roses together with our children.

5.

Acquiring A Sense Of Humor

How do parents do it? How do they make it through the hassles of raising a family? Seems there's a guiding spirit who tells us, "Hey, don't take life so seriously, have some fun, enjoy!" This good humor spirit keeps parents on track, helping them laugh when they really feel like crying.

Having a sense of humor is the greatest gift anyone can have. With it, parents become survivors; without it, life is a drag. Parents need to see the humor in their lives. They need to laugh at themselves, at the crazy situations they get into, and the insane conditions they put up with. A sense of humor relieves a tense situation to bring harmony to a family. Humor changes the way parents get through each day. It also determines the way parents handle small as well as large incidents, especially those that can make or break marriages and families.

Humor is essential. A sense of humor makes optimists out of pessimists. You simply can't look at life's situations with a sense of humor and remain a pessimist. For that reason, parents need to help their children acquire a sense of humor. With humor and an optimistic attitude, household jobs get lighter and easier for children, maybe even fun. What a good way to start children in life, and what a help to them later in adult jobs.

Given hindsight, events that seemed so serious at the time they happened are often recalled and retold with a sense of humor. One conclusion, therefore, seems appropriate: parents should think with hindsight when using foresight!

II. Early Mothering

6.

Children Just Fit

Isn't it amazing the way our bodies are made, how everything seems to fit together? How perfectly we've been designed to do all the things we need to do: the way our back bends, or the many ways our arms, legs, fingers and toes move. Consider also the functions of our bones, muscles, skin, eyelashes, brows, hair, hearts, brains, lungs, stomachs, eyes, nose, ears, mouths. Surely some Master Planner put this great specimen of ourselves together. We're not only able to interact with nature, including its animals, plants, and other wonders, but an expectant mother also shares her own body with the new life she carries. In view of the remarkable intelligence reflected in nature's designs, and in view of the complexity of every breath we take, is it really possible we could have just happened to exist? Our electrical system, our plumbing, all our life's systems are in their

17

proper places at birth. Our bodies are a kind of universe striving to keep the various parts in good working order.

Now think what happens after a child is born. Mother's arms bend at just the right spot for holding her infant. Her fingers and hands help to care for her baby at nap time, meal time, play time, and any other time. When she holds her baby in her arms to nurse, mother's breasts are in the best place to give her baby feedings of life-sustaining milk. And what about a mother's milk, which mysteriously comes only when it's needed?

Think about your knees. They bend to reach a child's level. When formed into a lap, they can hold a child. Consider also how a child is easily enclosed in loving arms; arms that serve children and family in so many ways.

Mother's hands serve to wash not only her children, but all their clothes, too. Then her hands lovingly fold the clothes, prepare meals, give first aid, pick up after everyone, clean the house, make the beds, prepare treats, comfort the sick and the sad, reach for life's necessities, change baby's diapers.... The list seems endless.

The wonders, the miracles of the human body and the universe are gifts to us all, not just an elite few. They're for the loved and the unloved, the wanted and the unwanted, the perfect and the imperfect. Nature plays no favorites.

We each have an obligation to care for and love the miraculous lives entrusted to us. No matter how these lives break down or wear out, they're to be loved and accounted for, because they're part of the universe, part of us. Also, our children should be taught to appreciate the priceless gift of their body, and how to use it with respect and dignity.

7.

Getting Into Parenting

Twenty or thirty years ago, most first-time mothers were in their late teens to early twenties. College graduation wasn't always expected of young women. Two years of college seemed enough, and if women hadn't found a husband by that time, they seemed destined to be old maids. As a result, child-bearing years were mostly confined to the twenties and early thirties.

The twenties have definite advantages. Bodies of women in their twenties are probably as strong and healthy as they will ever be. Energy level is usually much higher than it is in the forties. For that reason, the twenties seem to be a good, healthy time to have babies. As years pass and more children come, however, child bearing becomes more difficult for a mother's body. By the time her forties approach, her child-bearing years have usually ended.

Today, a new dimension has been added. Many first-time mothers are now in their late thirties and early forties. This raises new questions. Since these women are having their first babies at a much older age, is this an advantage or disadvantage? Is a forty-year-old mother endowed with more wisdom and patience because of her age? Or, for example, will she be short on patience and energy when dealing with an extremely active two-year-old? Do mothers lose or gain patience with age? It's wise for any woman contemplating motherhood to give it serious thought. A key question is: will the mother have sufficient love and self-sacrifice in her heart to adequately love and nurture her child?

Other questions having nothing to do with age are equally important for would-be mothers (fathers, too) to consider. For example, will a woman who's successful in a career be able to put her career aside? If she continues working, who will care for her child? Will this person act in the child's best interest? Also, why do would-be parents want a child? Will the child be a burden? Will the child be a joy? What do they expect of their child? What can their child expect of them? Are these expectations satisfactory?

One requirement, respect for parenthood, is essential. Would-be parents of all ages should treat parenthood with the awe, wonder, and humility it deserves. Parenting isn't easy. Nothing of great worth and value ever is. Rewards are only as great as the effort given to a job.

8.

Working Versus At-Home Mothers

There are at least two groups of working mothers employed outside the home on a daily basis. Mothers in the first group are trying to earn enough to survive. These moms haven't many alternatives. They're doing what they must do. Moms in the second group are employed outside the home to buy a second car, get a better home, wear newer clothes, finance a vacation, or, in general, live better than they could without the second income. A key question is, can a woman handle two careers and do justice to both? In other words, can she be both a successful career woman and career mother at the same time?

When children are pre-schoolers, a twenty-four-hour-a-day mom is important, not only for the children but also for mother. Young lives are so filled with opportunities for spontaneous celebration of "firsts": first smile, first turn-over, first step, first word, tooth, kiss, hug, response, and on and on. These "first" years produce most of the lifetime devotion and admiration between child and mother. Childhood demands a mother's time. She shouldn't miss the casual and unhurried play, walks, talks and leisurely companionship of her children that can occur on a twenty-four-hour basis.

The tendency today is to attempt to experience everything life has to offer *right now*. Yet, there's plenty of time for all things; we simply need to put priorities in proper order. A mother's goal is being the best mother she can be.

Mothers don't have to deny themselves opportunities to improve and grow. They do have to define what those words mean at any particular time of their lives. When children are young, for example, mothers have the brief opportunity to enjoy them. Why would mothers want to waste that opportunity? Their children will be in school soon enough. At that time, mothers can slip into the job market on a part-time basis if they're interested in doing that.

In the past twenty-five years, pre-school training patterns have changed dramatically. Nursery school wasn't common for pre-schoolers thirty years ago. Now, with so many nursery schools around, mothers wonder, "What's the hurry"? All that used to be required of children at the end of kindergarten was that they count to twenty-five. Now children have to read and start some new math program by that time. Why the rush? The social atmosphere of a child's kindergarten was of major importance in years past. Now a child's social atmosphere, with its communicable diseases, begins almost at birth in day care centers.

Our society is in conflict with its values. Many children have become little more than machines that are overloaded with fuel, and kept running continuously from home to school to day care center and back again. What are we doing to them? Their individualism and uniqueness have faded into the background. Children have become inconveniences that get in the way of a woman's professional career.

It seems that lack of good day care for children has burdened so many mothers with so much guilt that the money they earned to improve their quality of life is now being spent on psychologists, who are hired to get rid of the guilt that's destroying a family's quality of life.

Latch key kids are another present day phenomenon. Instead of coming home to parents to share their day, latch key children come home to an empty house, TV, abuse by older brothers and sisters, or other problems of unsupervised circumstances. Are parents rationalizing an unhealthy environment for their children? Are they being selfish and self-centered?

Families are dissolving; divorce is an accepted solution to almost every marital problem. Twenty-five years ago it wasn't. Is life happier now? Is there any justification for two incomes to get the material extras from life? Sacrifice of a child's love and welfare might be the price parents pay.

What are parents doing to their children's value system? What attitude will today's children have toward their own children? Will there be latch key children two or three years old in the next generation?

If parents have a choice, let them decide wisely and unselfishly whether, or when, mother should go to work outside the home. The good of their children must be parents' first priority.

9.

Nursing Baby

Obstetricians don't usually ask a mother before the birth of her child whether she intends to nurse. However, discussion of nursing should be part of a mother's prenatal care so she can make an informed decision about nursing before she's on the delivery table. Women like to be prepared. A mother-to-be, long before her delivery time, should be given positive information about breast and bottle feeding so that she can make the best decision for her and baby.

When a mother is working outside the home, bottle feeding her baby may be a necessity. Yet, there are some mothers who manage to breast feed their babies even though they're working. There are still other working mothers who both bottle feed and breast feed. If the first time a woman learns about breast feeding is in the hospital just after delivery, she won't be prepared and will probably be nervous about it.

If a new mother decides to nurse her baby, she faces other problems. For some reason, when people (usually the new mother's mother) find out that a new mother is breast feeding her baby, the first thing they tell her is how great it is. The second thing they do is try to talk her out of it. The third thing they do is put an ear near her breast while her child is nursing, to make sure the milk is flowing.

Some simple guides for mothers can help them become successful at nursing, but primarily they should relax and enjoy it. They should view nursing as a time to do some reading, close their eyes and catch a few winks, or simply enjoy their baby and the bonding that's happening. They can be happy they didn't have to sterilize a bottle, prepare a formula, or clean up the mess afterwards.

I have to smile every time I remember the birth of our last child. I had just turned forty, had ample gray hair, and needed a little boost to my morale. So before delivery I dyed my hair (I didn't want to look like the kid's grandma), and my husband ordered a private room. One would think that with seven other children waiting for me at home, I would enjoy a private room. I did, but I requested that the baby be in my room all the time. With our other children eagerly waiting for us at home, the time that my new baby and I would have alone together was brief and precious. A peaceful, restful, hospital setting, though brief, gets nursing off to a good start.

A mother can read technical books to find out about the excellent nourishment of breast milk. Not only is it great for her baby, but once she gets used to breast feeding, she and baby will love it. It's so easy. All a mother has to do is snuggle up in bed at 2:00 a.m. with her baby next to her. That's comfort!

For about six months it usually isn't necessary to feed a baby cereal or anything else other than breast milk. How inspiring it is to realize that naturally, through the use of a mother's own body, which was designed to produce milk after birth, she and she alone is giving her baby life, and she alone is the means by which her baby will *grow*, and gain weight and height. By way of reward, a baby, when nursing, helps tighten mother's stomach muscles and return her uterus to its proper shape. Baby even helps mother lose weight. What a team! Both mother and baby grow healthier by means of the simple and natural act of nursing.

10.

Doctoring

We each have our share of sickness in childhood years. It seems children have a bad year, build up a few immunities, then have a couple of good years. Calling a doctor at any time of day or night is common for a new, inexperienced parent worried about a tiny, helpless little human being. A human baby is totally dependent on mother for so long a time, and can't talk for so long after birth, that mother usually has to seek a doctor's advice.

When a mother is more experienced with minor illnesses she'll be able to take care of her child until a doctor can be reached during office hours. She'll probably have to do that anyway. If she calls her doctor in the middle of the night, she'll usually be told to call the office in the morning and make an appointment. If a situation is really bad, her only alternative is to go directly to a hospital emergency room. Her doctor can meet her there.

Today isn't like the good old days of doctor's house calls. Also, during daytime hours, it's difficult to find a doctor willing to give instructions over the phone. A nurse at the doctor's office usually says, "Bring the child in."

"But he's too sick to go out in 20° below zero weather," protests the mother.

"Then take him to the hospital," advises the nurse, impatiently.

We're dealing with doctors who, for good reasons, won't diagnose over the telephone. They're worried about the prospect of expensive malpractice lawsuits. Nevertheless, a few words said in a helpful, sincere way can ease a mother's fears.

Our pediatrician once commented to me that he hardly ever saw me. It wasn't that our kids were always so healthy, but that I was able to treat most of the common diseases or cuts and bruises they got. For example, if the flu goes around and our child gets it, I'm going to keep the child home and provide home treatment rather than force the flu-sick child into -20° weather for a trip to the doctor's office, where the only thing the doctor will do is diagnose that the child has the flu.

Keep in mind, we're only talking about common medical problems. It's wonderful to have a helpful neighbor or friend whose children have had the common illnesses. Basically, a mother should remain calm and use good sense. Yet, it's so hard when your baby cries and you don't know why.

Earaches especially are devils. The best a mother can do sometimes is simply comfort her fussy baby.

When you think of the ordeal babies endure just being born, you have to believe there might be a few touchy nerve endings. Also, it takes so little snuggling and soothing to comfort babies, and the bond formed by doing that seems to grow so much stronger. When a baby communicates in the only way babies can, by crying, be ready to assume something is wrong, then offer all the comfort you can.

11.

Feeding Toddlers

At a restaurant table next to the one where my husband and I were sitting, there was a girl about two years old with her mother and grandmother. As the drama unfolded, everyone's attention turned to those three.

The two-year-old girl was obviously enjoying her outing. This particular restaurant didn't have children's portions, so she was served a generous adult portion of hamburger and fries. Halfway through her meal, the child slowed down. Her little tummy was full. Rather than let the little girl end her meal on a happy note, however, Grandma started in. "If you don't eat all your food, you can't have any animal cookies!"

The little girl began to get upset. Grandma stood firm and repeated her ultimatum three more times while mother remained silent.

The little girl started to cry. The more upset she became the harder she cried. The harder she cried, the more Grandma threatened. Mother still didn't say anything.

The little girl's tears were now being observed by others in the restaurant. To silence her, Grandma threatened again. Then she told the girl's mother that the child had been ornery all day. By this time the child had become hysterical and was out of control. She was sobbing whole-heartedly.

Grandma said, "The trouble is, it's past her nap time and she's crabby!"

Still, mother said nothing. What started out as a happy outing and special treat, became a nightmare for the little girl.

Finally, Grandma reversed her threat. "Stop crying, the animal cookies are in the car," she said.

The rest of the child's lunch was put into a doggie bag *along with the rest of mother's lunch, because even mother couldn't finish a large, identical serving.* To an observer, it was like being at the Mad Hatter's Tea Party.

Anyone served too much food shouldn't have to eat it. Also, even if a meal isn't completely eaten, a sweet for dessert can still taste good.

12.

The Terribly Wonderful Two's

Notice that the word "Wonderful" is inserted between "Terribly" and "Two's." Many moms respond in a positive way to the two's, because children at that age are so much fun. Children seem to learn so quickly then. Each day is exciting to anticipate.

What new experience will there be? What a privilege it is to share moments of discovery and help baby safely try new things. Walking and talking are both usually taking place at this time, and if there are older brothers and sisters, they're now being put in their place. No more is the gutsy two-year-old so eager to be the "go-fer." Older children are simply told "no" by the newly aware two-year-old. It's as if overnight our Creator reached down and infused a free will into the tiny tykes.

However, the new-found independence causes trouble with other family members, especially mom and dad. For two years this little child has been like clay, soft and pliable, ready for parents to mold. Now, all of a sudden, a sense of self-importance, free will, independence, and the urge to explore, have developed.

If a mother is a respectful and loving parent, the two's shouldn't be too difficult. She might actually relax a little with her two-year-old, because now the toddler is at last beginning to understand a *little*. Also, the two's seem to signal an end to the exhausting chores of caring for a baby.

There's one other time before the age of two that's also a turning point. It's a baby's first smile. Before babies are able to smile, their faces often look troubled. They seem so much older, as if they carry great burdens. Then one day a smile lights up their face, and they really and truly look like babies instead of worried old people. Baby's smile seems to put an end to mother's anxieties and intimidation.

As children get older, mothers should look back through photo albums and take a special look at those pictures taken when their children were two years old. At that age children are so beautiful and angelic looking. Their cherub-like faces may never look sweeter, nor their bodies more lovely. Looking through picture albums at happy two year olds is enough to bring tears to a mom's eyes, and usually does.

13.

Creating A Scene

Most mothers have been with their children in a public place when, for one reason or another, a child becomes upset and creates a scene. It doesn't matter if it's in a crowded restaurant, bus, department store, church, or park. Whenever it happens, it's embarrassing to parents. How nice it would be if people would simply look the other way for a few minutes so parents can escape their embarrassment gracefully.

Usually we sympathize with parents when a stubborn child creates a scene in public. However, a recent situation in a local department store had everyone sympathizing with the child. As I came into the store I passed a mother who was anxiously trying to stop her toddler from crying. She was on her knees speaking eye to eye with him, and saying she would have to take him home if he didn't quit crying. All this to no avail. There was no reasoning with him; he was so young.

I walked to the department I was headed for, which was at the far end of the store. Taking my time, I looked for clothes, decided what items to try on, tried them on, made my selections, and paid for them. All that time I could hear the same child crying at the other end of the store. He was getting hysterical. I walked past him again on the way to my car to put my new clothes in the trunk. When I returned, the toddler was still crying.

Next, I went to a nearby store, made more purchases, returned to my car via the same route and, alas, there they were again, the mother talking, the child still crying. For over an hour that helpless toddler kept crying. The question is not only how can a child possibly cry that long while standing up, without falling asleep out of sheer exhaustion, but how could his mother refuse to pick him up and comfort him or take him home? How long must the boy be crying at home, if he's allowed to cry so long in a public place, in the presence of a store full of annoyed customers who are forced to become a reluctant audience?

The mother told her little boy that she would take him home if he continued to cry. The child continued to cry, but the mother didn't follow through on her promise to take him home. When a child cries like that, something is wrong. The problem could be as simple as a wet diaper, a developing rash, a hungry tummy or a tired body.

There's usually a good reason why children cry. Mothers should be alert to the urgent needs that cause crying, then try to satisfy those needs.

14.

Planning Anticipation

The best part of Christmas comes before December 25. The most fun of a birthday is the time just before the big event. An upcoming luncheon date or party is enjoyed for a week or more before it happens. The best part of any event is usually the anticipation. Watching children prepare for Halloween brings back many fond memories of one's own childhood. Weeks were spent deciding and preparing who to look like. One little girl's costume always ended up the same every year—Mae West. She didn't know much about Mae West, but she knew it meant dressing up and wearing makeup, and that's all she cared about.

Sometimes Halloween began with a party, which made the evening even more fun, because it gave us more to anticipate. But the party wasn't enjoyed for long. Soon we were anxiously waiting for the big excitement of getting handouts. When we got home and sorted our loot of candy and stuff, it wasn't nearly as much fun as we had anticipating it the day before.

Everyone needs something to anticipate, something exciting to get adrenalin flowing. Just the anticipation of an exciting upcoming event, a new job, or better times, for example, can be enough to help those who are hurting get through unpleasant times. People need something pleasant to look forward to, rather than their past hurts to brood on.

Surprise parties can be fun once or twice in a lifetime, but not too often. The reason is that they deprive us of anticipation, which is the best part of a party.

How fun it is for parents to plan events for children to anticipate. The event need not be big or costly. For example, it's fun for kids to hear before they leave for school that they'll have freshly-baked cookies waiting for them when they get home. Or, if the weather is going to be nice after school, it's fun for them to know that mother will take them for a pleasant walk to the park. Or, if every Friday night is set aside as family night with a popcorn party, it's fun for children to anticipate it. Maybe if the weekend weather will be good, you can let your children anticipate that you'll take them for a ride around some lake, go to the zoo, or pick apples. If you're having a great favorite for supper, tell your children about it before they leave for school so they can anticipate it all day. If you're going on a summer vacation, talk it up for the whole year to give the children plenty of anticipation time.

One of the nicest gifts parents give their children is the gift of anticipation. It's such a thoughtful gift, too, one that children can pass on to their own children someday. Anticipation can begin a tradition as well as become a happy memory. Anticipation is worth planning.

15.

Being Creative

There's a growing group of stay-home mothers. "Growing" is the right word, because these mothers, once vanishing, are getting easier to find. They're the ones staying home to take care of their pre-school children. For that reason, these mothers don't want to work at a paying job outside the home.

While most women today are part of a stimulating job environment, mothers who stay home all day cleaning, washing, and scrubbing, are also in an environment of young children who speak only one and two syllable words. Such an environment gives these stay-home mothers a great need to be creative. Fortunately, there are many creative activities these women can enjoy.

In a world of fast foods and supermarkets, for example, one fulfilling activity can be the slower pace of yesteryear's home-baked bread. There's nothing quite like the smooth, elastic feel of bread dough being kneaded under the palms of mother's hands, or the feel of creativity she gets after the mixing, setting, and raising of sweet rolls, then forming them into traditional shapes. Following a recipe to bake a cake from scratch, or rolling out a pie crust, can be surprisingly fulfilling work. Creativity of this sort is much more satisfying than opening a box mix or buying something baked by someone else. Even though it may be consumed by delighted children in a very short time, mother will still have had the pleasure of creating something grand.

What about creating other kinds of beauty for the family: a picture for a wall, new curtains, homemade clothes, painting or papering a room, refinishing a piece of furniture, planting a garden, raking a yard and sprucing it up? The rewards of a mother's creativity will come back to her in many surprising ways through her children, and her children will someday pay her the ultimate compliment, imitation.

III. Sigh-cology of Mothering

16.

Developing A Positive Approach

There are two ways to answer questions requiring a yes or no answer: "Yes" or "No." Too many "No" answers can cause children to become discouraged and acquire a negative outlook on life. With a little effort, however, you can give a negative response in a positive way. Simply think up an approach that will encourage the positive behavior you want.

Kids receiving negative replies come away discouraged. If you must give a negative reply, try putting a positive twist to it. For example, when a child asks for a piece of candy right before supper, you would ordinarily use either the negative approach or the positive approach.

Negative Approach

CHILD: "Mom, can I have a piece of candy?"
MOM: "No, you'll ruin your supper!"

Positive Approach

CHILD: "Mom, can I have a piece of candy?"
MOM: "Yes, right after supper!"

Subtle or not, the positive approach works. Kids invariably reply, "OK!" and scoot off happily. Consider the positive approach in a few other examples.

Movie Request

CHILD: "Mom, can I go to a movie tonight?"
MOM: "Yes, if you get an early start and get home by 10:00." Rather than: "No, you'll be home too late."

Guest Request

CHILD: "Mom, can I have Mary over?"
MOM: "Yes, let's plan on next Tuesday." Rather than: "No, I'm busy tonight."

Pierced Ears Request

CHILD: "Mom, can I get my ears pierced?"
MOM: "Yes, when you're in eighth grade." Rather than: "No, you're too young."

Request for Help

CHILD TO HARRIED TEACHER: "I can't do this problem."

TEACHER: "I'll be happy to explain it to you...
1) during recess."
2) when I finish what I'm doing."
3) after school." Rather than: "No, I don't
have time now."

Child's Complaint

CHILD TO TEACHER: "You gave me two
demerits, and all I did was look around at
the noise in the back of the room."
TEACHER: "I'm sorry. You're correct. I should
have only given you one demerit, and if you
feel that was unfair I will be happy to
discuss it with you after class. Rather than:
"Don't look around!"

Sleep-over Request

CHILD: "Can Billy sleep over?" (Billy standing
right there!)
MOM: "Yes, we'll work it out for next week"
("month," "year"). Rather than: "No, we're
having grandma and grandpa tonight."

Request to Play Outside

CHILD: "May I go out and play?"
MOM: "Yes, as soon as you finish your
homework" ("practice," "clean your room,"
"set table," etc.). Rather than: "No, you
have too much work to do."

Got the idea? A positive approach is quite simple, but requires some
practice to make it automatic.

Of course, sometimes a firm, direct "no" is necessary. With a positive approach, however, it's surprising how seldom "no" is needed.

A sense of humor also helps. An eldest daughter gave her mother a great deal of trouble over curfews. On her eighteenth birthday she boldly announced, "Now that I'm eighteen, my curfew is going to be 2:00 a.m." To which her mother replied, "Fine, where are you going to live?"

When one child has a grievance against a younger brother or sister, and asks *why* the parents had so many children, try a little innocent humor. If the complaining child, for instance, is your fourth child, say, "Yes, Dad and I originally wanted only three children." That's usually enough to end the discussion.

When one of her sons (at the ripe age of sixteen) called his mother a "bitch" in a stage whisper once too often, she asked him a simple question. "If I'm a 'bitch,' does that make you a 'son of a bitch' or a 'bastard'?"

Since your negativism isn't working, anyway, what have you got to lose? Think positive!

17.

Spanking And Name-Calling

A family is a blessing in so many ways. One way is that it keeps parents so busy they either mellow or die of exhaustion. When parents have their first child, in their enthusiasm for excellence, they sometimes spank the child for being naughty. As more children come, however, parents begin to realize that spanking simply releases the anger of the "spanker." It does nothing to solve the problem of the "spankee." Usually, as parents become more experienced, they learn that spankings are not only dangerous, but they're unnecessary for raising good children.

Comparing spanked with unspanked kids, parents may see very little difference. All their kids are equally naughty or nice. Rather than spank their first ones, therefore, parents could simply have sat them on their beds, as they may have done with the later ones. Perhaps it could have saved everyone a lot of trouble.

The alternatives of sending misbehaving children to their room or "grounding" them, accomplishes similar results as spanking, but there aren't such hard feelings afterwards. Children are usually the first to realize when they've done something wrong. They don't need to have it pounded into them.

The same is true with name-calling. A child has a strong sense of justice and realizes when punishment is deserved. Parents don't need to call their children names to remind them of the nature of an offense. Chances are, the children have already called themselves a few names. Children punish themselves enough. Parents don't need to add to the punishment.

Would parents raise their hand in anger to a friend or stranger? Would they call their best friend a name? Would they call a stranger a name? Would they themselves like to be called a name? Would parents like to be whipped for having their own opinion of something if it differs from someone else's?

It's never too late for parents to change their ways and apologize to their kids if they were wrong. Then parents and children can treat each other with renewed respect. Children love their parents and can forgive them, no matter how unfair or human their parents act. And parents can profit from their children's good example by being more *tolerant* of children when they fail.

18.

Getting Children To Bed

A child psychologist led a guided discussion at a recent PTA workshop. The answer he gave to a question from a concerned mother created considerable controversy among many of the experienced mothers present. The question from the concerned mother was this: "Bedtime has become a hassle for me. My children think up a million excuses not to go to bed at night and a million more to get out of bed as soon as they're in it. I yell and scream, spank, threaten, and end up a mental wreck every time. What should I do?"

The woman was visibly upset. Her kids were enjoying the big show every night. So what did the psychologist recommend? "Firm discipline." The lady said she had done that, but bedtime was still a drag.

Perhaps if she hadn't gone by the book and avoided confrontation and the firm discipline approach, she might have had better results. Before her children go to bed, she could, for example, try giving them a "party." Now, that doesn't mean baking a cake with candles or having presents.

The word "party" is used very loosely. It might consist simply of some fruit, cheese, candy, cookies, milk, hot chocolate, crackers or whatever a mother's vivid imagination can dream up. Remember,it's a *simple* treat. If children know they'll have a party before bedtime, and that afterwards they're expected to go upstairs, wash, brush their teeth, and get into bed, then their bedtime will become a good time. Also, as soon as they're in bed, you can bring them a drink of water and kiss them good night. Any trouble, no more parties. Everyone goes to bed happy, including mother.

Don't worry that this bedtime party approach will grow into a lifetime habit unable to be broken. Children will naturally drift away from it when they're older. They'll have homework and other chores and interests.

Since everyone enjoys happy children, mothers may want to subscribe to the theory, "It if feels comfortable and right, it probably is; if it doesn't feel right, don't do it." One of the stronger tendencies of any mother should be to trust her common sense.

The key to cooperative behavior is simple. *Assume* children will behave in a proper manner and they usually will. Mother's love for them is transmitted by her unhurried and sharing attitude. She's not forcing them to get attention by negative behavior. They feel her love in her unhurried, happy ending to their day.

19.

Running Away

If you have a child more than a few years old, you've probably dealt with the runaway routine. Usually parents are informed of the upcoming event. Sometimes they even participate in the preparations. If not, what's the fun of it for the children?

One runaway incident in our household occurred with two of our daughters. I don't recall what prompted it, but the girls planned it for most of the morning. Clothes were packed, as well as treasures and items needed for what was to apparently be a long journey. Since we had a large wooden playhouse in our backyard, the girls included it in their plans. They packed books to read as well as games to play. However, they forgot the most important thing they needed: their lunch.

Although I knew the girls were in the playhouse, I didn't realize the significance of their mission. It was no surprise that when 12:00

noon came, the girls showed up for lunch. However, it was years later, when all the kids were sharing stories about how they put things over on me, that I found out they were disappointed because I didn't even know they had run away. Maybe that's why our younger children became more vocal: they wanted to be sure their parents got the message.

Another family incident wasn't an official runaway-from-home affair, because our three-year-old son told his father where he was going. He was going to church to find his mom. At three years old, my husband didn't take him seriously. Here's what happened.

As I was leaving for an 11:00 a.m. service that Sunday, my three-year-old son asked me if he could come with me. It was too late to clean him up and get him ready, so I said I would take him another time. After I left, he told his father he was going to church.

Later, when I came home and asked where he was, my husband said he was in the yard playing. That upset me, because my husband, who was inside reading the Sunday paper, couldn't possibly have been watching our son who was outside. We looked and called and searched in vain. Then we got the neighbors looking with us. Finally, the telephone rang. An usher at our church, which was over a mile away, phoned to tell us that our son had just arrived (it took him an hour and a half to get there), and was looking for his mother. What a shock! Our son not only had to walk for over a mile to get there, he also had to cross several busy intersections and dodge heavy traffic. We didn't know how he knew the way, and, in fact, we finally decided he probably didn't, since it took him an hour and a half to get there! He probably got lost a number of times.

When I arrived at the church, I hugged and kissed my little boy as only a frantic and relieved mother could. Then, in a calm but miffed voice he said, "I *told* you I wanted to go to church."

Eventually, life in our large family reached the point that when a child got upset with me, I took my apron off, suggested the child stay home, and I could run away for awhile. The arrangement seems much more practical that way.

20

Settling Arguments

What's one of the toughest jobs a parent has to deal with? If you said being judge and jury, you're right. If you said being judge and jury when you haven't seen anything happen, you win the prize.

What to do about the "tattle-tale" kid causes a real dilemma. A child shouldn't be punished for walking away from trouble and telling a parent what happened. And yet, to listen to the chronic teller of tales is to encourage tattle-tale behavior until it becomes unbearable.

Based on experience, there are at least two stock answers that seem to be successful in ending a lot of trouble. Parents can use them over and over again. The answers will probably serve their purpose for many years to come. It takes kids years to realize what parents are doing, but when the dawn finally comes, children tell parents the offense, hesitate, then immediately answer their own request, or solve their own problem..

Stock Answer No. 1

The first stock answer is used when a parent is confronted by two angry children demanding a solution to their argument. Example:

FIRST CHILD:	"I was playing with the ball and he took it away from me!"
SECOND CHILD:	"I found it in the grass and no one was around."
PARENT:	"I'm sorry, I wasn't there. I didn't see it. I can't judge what happened."

Stock Answer No. 2

Stock answer two takes a different twist. Only one child comes storming in with a problem for a parent to solve. The parent has no previous knowledge of the problem.

CHILD:	"Billy slugged me!"
PARENT:	"Don't play with him anymore."
CHILD:	"Mary stole my friend!"
PARENT:	"Don't play with her anymore."

"Don't play with her anymore" accomplishes miracles. The first thing the offended child does is turn around and go right back to play with the supposed culprit. Sometimes the child is so surprised, he or she will even defiantly tell the parent, "Yes, I will!"

One line recently used by a mother is a prize winner. When her two children got down to the last cookie in the cookie jar, they began fighting over who should get it. Mom walked up to the jar, grabbed the cookie, put it in her mouth, and said in a garbled voice as she walked away, "No one ever said life was fair!"

21

Avoiding Trouble

From early childhood children should be told to keep far away from trouble. They shouldn't stand around and watch it. They shouldn't laugh or encourage troublemakers. They should keep right on moving. It's almost certain that someone watching from a nearby window will see *part* of what's happening, so that when an innocent child is seen anywhere near the trouble, that child will be reported right along with the others.

Trouble attracts kids like bees to nectar. When a couple of kids get into fights, they draw a crowd. If a street light gets shot out, and your child is part of the group of observers, your child, if seen and recognized, will be assumed to be as guilty as the rest. People might not be able to tell who actually shot out the light. Rather, the group as a whole is guilty. If a teacher leaves the room and three kids start a ruckus, it's not at all unusual for the whole class to be punished for the disturbance.

It's a good lesson for later in life as well. How many innocent people have been imprisoned on circumstantial evidence? They just happened to be in the wrong spot at the wrong time, maybe watching trouble happen instead of getting someone to stop it.

The same is true for loitering. If kids are going to loiter, better they do it at a friend's house. Otherwise it can be very dangerous.

An incident that happened to one family with two boys, ages five and six, taught a long-lasting lesson. Since the stories of the two little boys never varied, even when they were much older, they were believable. One day the two brothers were walking down the alley near their home to call on one of their friends. They were taking their time on the way back home. Later that day, the boys' mother got a call from a woman at the end of the alley, whose backyard fence ran along one side of the alley. It seemed a corner fence post had been knocked down, and, according to her account, another neighbor told her the boys did it. The neighbor had assumed the boys were guilty, merely because they were seen walking in the area.

It was unlikely that such small boys could break a ten-inch thick fence post, but, unfortunately, their parents couldn't *prove* they didn't. All they could do was tell the neighbor that their boys said they didn't do it. However, since the parents couldn't *prove* their boys' innocence, the boys' father had to "volunteer" to come down with the boys to fix the neighbor's fence.

As it turned out, the fence post was so completely rotted through, it had probably recently fallen over. Therefore, the boys' father had a sizable repair job on his hands. The complaining neighbor, on the other hand, apparently saw an opportunity to have a rotted fence repaired free. While the boys felt bad for their dad, the deeper lesson they learned about the world's injustice will be with them for a long time. It's also a good lesson to all of us not to rash judge. What we *think* we see may not be what we're actually seeing.

A group of kids waiting for a friend to show up may be rash-judged as loiterers, waiting for trouble to happen. Innocent, underaged kids walking around a lake may be approached by other underaged kids, not so innocent, one of whom has a bottle of liquor.

If police suddenly show up, the innocent become one with the guilty and all get punished. Your child's "friend" may turn out to be a shoplifter who gets caught when your child just happens to be along, not knowing about his shoplifting friend. The result? Your child, though innocent, gets arrested as an accomplice.

No one said life was fair, but parents were given brains, instincts, and common sense to protect themselves and their children. What they need to do now is train themselves and their children to use these mental gifts. Parents need to help their children be alert to questionable circumstances so they can be avoided; and to expect the unexpected, so appropriate action can be taken to eliminate trouble.

22

One More DOES Matter

Busy mothers, especially mothers with many children, have occasionally had other mothers tell them, "With all your kids, one more for a few hours won't matter." Then they push little Joey in the door and skedaddle. It's unfortunate such behavior is so prevalent. Culprits who use the line, "one more doesn't matter," should be asked, why, then, if one more doesn't matter, don't they take their little Joey right along with them to wherever they're going?

Maybe a mother wants to get her hair done or run an errand, and needs another mother to watch her Joey for just two hours. Will she let that other mother drop off her own gang of kids when she needs to do something?

Assume the noise level is relatively moderate in the house where Joey is visiting. Then, without being invited, Joey wanders into Billy's bedroom and starts rummaging through Billy's toys. That's when the trouble starts. Big families usually have great respect for each other's property, because space and a child's treasures are limited. That's why children in the same family avoid taking each other's toys or possessions without an "OK" from the owner. Unfortunately, after emptying Billy's toy box, Joey starts on the book shelf; after the book shelf, the closet. Now Billy is upset.

Since guest explorer Joey has begun to find some excitement in the hunt, he goes to Sally's room next. Sally gets upset. Soon mom is upset as well, because Billy and Sally can't be expected to clean Joey's mess, and mom already has enough to do.

Perhaps visitor Joey is a great little guy, almost no bother at all. He just has to stay for supper. But let's assume mom hasn't had any notice, since that's usually how it happens. Tonight she's planned a pork chop dinner. Since the exact number of pork chops had been purchased, each child, plus mom and dad, get one pork chop to eat. What happens now? Mom's pork chop goes to guest Joey, while mom looks vulturously at her youngest child repeating every 10 seconds, "All done? Let me clear your plate!"

If it isn't an afternoon or dinner time scenario, let's say guest Joey comes in the evening. Dad arrives home from a hard day's work. After a nice supper, he decides to sprawl in front of the TV and relax. Too bad, visitor Joey is in Dad's favorite chair. Dad then suggests that Joey might like to accompany Billy on the huge davenport, where there's also room for at least three other children. Joey, however, declines because he likes it where he is. Too bad for dad.

All families, especially big families, more than any other group in the world, need time alone together as a family whenever they can. Often it's no easy task to sit everyone down at the same table. Family times are times to be cherished, and a family's private space is extremely important. The uninvited Joeys of the world make matters more difficult. Don't add to their job. Whether visiting a small family or large family, one extra child in a home is more work. One more *does* matter!

23

Big Family Mothering

The more children parents have, the more parents mellow. If they don't, they could lose their minds. Any mom with a large number of children has to mellow, take shortcuts, and not let interruptions upset her. If she let the increasing activity, noise, and frustrations overwhelm her, she might not be able to survive motherhood.

My sister-in-law once commented to me that with our eight children, "Every meal is a banquet." She could be right! However, my children leave for school at different times, so they get their own breakfasts during the week. Also, they're quite capable of putting a sandwich or two together for lunch.

My children sometimes get frustrated because I don't rush in to solve all their problems or settle all their arguments. Occasionally, I give my opinion if asked, but my first reaction is to let the kids solve their own problems whenever possible. It's good training for them now, and important preparation for the future.

It wasn't always that way. At first I was the producer, director, stage manager and actor in the family drama. God in his great wisdom allowed me to have eight children, I'm certain, so that the first ones could have some breathing space. Bless the first ones who bore the burden of my over-zealous perfection program for everyone but mom. I was determined my children would be so perfect, that people who met them would marvel at their perfection...and also at their mother's zeal. Now, in my mellow years, I simply love my children for themselves. They don't need to constantly prove their worth. That's not to say there are no conflicts. There are. Many tears have been shed, both theirs and mine. Forgiveness is an everyday occurrence when people are allowed to make their own mistakes and profit by them.

It's fun to watch the relationships between older and younger children in big families. The younger children give teenagers the opportunity to express their love in many ways, either by hugging and caring, or helping and sharing. Love shows up in ways teenagers don't usually use to express themselves, especially when playing and talking with younger brothers and sisters. Younger children flower under such love and attention from older children. Such shared love is a real bonus in big families. Kids still argue among themselves, but they always protect and defend each other against troublemaking outsiders.

Also, big families respect the property of others, because they learn this respect within themselves. As a rule, it usually isn't the children from large families who carve their names in desks or destroy other property. Nor do they have so many personal possessions that they become insensitive to them. They also aren't careless with their clothes, because they probably bought them with their own savings.

Big families have taken lots of abuse from the world in general. How they survived the anti-big-family period of "replacing ourselves only" is a real miracle. The heckling and sneers got so bad that many mothers refused to go to the grocery accompanied by more than one or two children. Not only were glares at larger families icy, the stage whispers were devastating to moms and dads as well as kids. One commercial airline pilot told the father of a large family that his big family was polluting the pilot's environment. The pilot, however, never considered what his airplane was doing to the family's environment!

At the present time, having more than two children now seems more acceptable. When big families go out together these days, not only are they smiled at, they're often stopped and complimented.

It's like the old joke about the hat but in reverse. The fellow in trouble throws his hat inside the door before he steps inside, as a kind of test to see if he's welcome. If his hat gets tossed out, he knows he's still in trouble, so he picks up his hat, puts it on, and leaves. When big families open the door to go *outside,* maybe they should toss their hats out first to see if it's OK for them to come out.

Big families must be extra special, since they're always on trial. The world seems to make them continually prove their merit. Large families take a lot of abuse from society and are a lot of hard work, no matter how mom has mellowed, but the rewards are also proportionally greater.

24

Next Door Neighbor Kid

One of the nicest things that can happen to a child is living next door to a best friend. The relationship that begins this way, at a young age, and is fortunate enough to continue through life, is so special that it's never quite equaled by any other friendship. It's really similar to a blood relationship. Maybe it's so special because it's comfortable, and formed before a child has any serious inhibitions.

Next door neighbor kids share secrets so dear to the heart that parents aren't even aware of them. When we were young, my best friend and I built tents and played house, school, or whatever our imaginations thought up. Sometimes our play didn't last very long, because arguments broke out and tents got knocked down. Our parents didn't interfere, and we were usually back together again soon, playing as though nothing happened.

Card games in the house or on a blanket in summer were popular with us, or reading in our favorite tree, or picking apples. An attic in

61

my best friend's house was a special wonderland. Now, they're almost non-existent. Our limit to having fun was in direct relationship to the limit of our imaginations. What glorious, carefree fun we used to have.

My next door neighbor and best friend was Diana. We were inseparable, and although we went to different elementary schools, we could hardly wait to get home each day to call for each other. Diana and my mom laughed years later when they reminisced about all the fights we used to have. It's funny, but I didn't remember any of them.

I REMEMBER...MY DEAR BEST FRIEND

Playing house and other games,
Climbing trees and reading in our favorite tree,
Sleeping out in our jungle hammocks,
Stealing apples,
Soaping windows on Halloween,
Spending holidays together,
Joining neighborhood games,
Going to Saturday movie matinees,
Running errands,
Swiping homemade cookies,
Ditching her cousin,
Taking care of her baby brother when we were 12,
Writing and illustrating a story,
Playing "Sally and Jane,"
Training our dogs,
Being world famous photographers,
Sucking nectar from lilacs,

Working in the yard,
Selling lemonade,
Sitting on chairs by the curb and counting the cars
    that waved to us,
Double dating,
Riding in a rumble seat,
Pledging the same high school sorority,
And having so many other wonderful times together.
My dear best friend, how we loved each other.

After our weddings our lives grew apart. We lived in different cities. When my husband and I moved back to town many years later, I phoned my friend Diana. It was like we had never been apart. Our conversation began in the same familiar way we left it years before. But circumstances had changed. Diana was very ill with diabetes. She had gotten the disease in her twenties, and by her late thirties she was a very sick woman. She was also a very courageous woman, who at one point in her suffering asked her husband, "Why does it take so long to die?" I was able to be with Diana at the end of her life—not at the last moment, because she died in her sleep in the middle of the night, but in her last months and days.

Diana gave so much, and very seldom, if ever, did she complain about her difficult life. She never had what she wanted most, children; but she and her husband were very good to ours. We all loved Diana and her husband.

Diana died at the young age of 42 years. I believe she is alive in another plane of existence, free of her diseased body. I feel that her spirit is soaring, and her happiness is great. Love you, next door neighbor kid! Thanks for all the wonderful memories, and for enriching my life in so many ways.

IV. Children's Views

25

Children Love...Children Hate

Did you ever think about some of the things children love or hate? One day I asked a group of kids to make two lists: one for things they love; one for things they hate. The surprise was that the love list came out fast, while the hate list took a long, long time. I wonder if the same would be true for adults, or, whether at their ripe age, the hate list would come out faster than the love list.

Here are the two lists, starting with the love list, since that was by far the more popular with the children. Seeing these two lists can give mothers some insight into the loving, open minds and hearts of children, so that children can be better understood.

CHILDREN LOVE ...

Anticipating surprises,
Parties,
Family nights,
Smell of baking when opening the front door,
Praise,
Helping ourselves,
Security,
Routine,
Fishing,
Pretending,
Treats,
Bright colors,
New shoes,
Walks,
Picnics,
Mom and dad being there,
Holidays,
Tradition,
Summer vacations,
Dependability,
Peer groups,
Pierced ears,
Our own rooms,
Stereos,
Telephones,
Clothes and jewelry,
Bicycles,
Sports,
Stories,

Pets,
Sliding,
Skating,
Sunny days,
Gardens,
Running through the hose,
April Fool's Day,
Drawing,
Gum,
Dressing up and playing dress-up,
TV,
Learning,
Camping,
Swimming,
Playing,
Eating popcorn or chocolate,
Getting and giving presents,
Climbing trees,
Parks,
Sandboxes,
Swings,
Clubs,
Board and card games,
Outside games,
Playing cars,
Playing dolls,
Thunderstorms when we're inside with the family,
Dandelions,
Staying up late,
Movies,
Sleep-overs,
Computers,
Picking apples,
Zoos,
Fairs,

Planting a garden,
Banging pans,
Corn on the cob,
Ice cream,
Grandparents,
Air conditioning,
Popsicles when sick,
Ice cream cones when well,
Getting better when sick,
Hot chocolate on cold days,
Sailing toothpick boats in puddles,
Hugs and kisses,
Magic,
Birthdays,
Being happy,
Surprises,
Night lights,
Competition,
Running,
Music,
Telling ghost stories,
Roasting marshmallows around a campfire,
Tricking people,
Blankets and thumbs,
Making parents happy.

CHILDREN HATE ...

School,
Going to bed,
Getting up early for school,
Bees,
Mosquitos,
Most vegetables,
Sand on roads when biking,
Absent parents,
Being bored
Going to bed after scary movies,
Bullies,
Unreasonableness,
Teasing,
Boring talks,
Church services,
Classes,
Any events not geared to us,
Throwing up,
Practicing,
Punishment–spankings and groundings,
Homework,
Being alone,
Having no friends,
Put downs,
Being car sick,
Being responsible,
Being embarrassed,
Getting caught in the rain,
Being scared,
Working,
Not being able to eat before supper when we're
    starving,
Getting into trouble,

Being thirsty,
Being sad and mad,
Blowing noses,
Being sick,
When feet fall asleep,
Nagging parents,
Braces,
Dumb questions,
Fighting with sisters and brothers,
When parties are over.

26

Children's Notes

Having heard that love and hate are closely related, its revealing to read some actual notes and letters from kids to moms. Some children are note-writers more than others, so what is presented here doesn't presume to represent all children. Also, the notes are reproduced faithfully in the manner they were written.

The greatest compliment

> Dear Mom,
>   I love you. You are my pal. I love you a lot. You are the greatest just like Grandma.
>
> > Bye know,
> > Love Ellen

Let's be reasonable, Mom

Dear Mom,
    I wish you would let me go outside. I don't have
a cold. I don't even know what you are talking
about. I just think you are freaking out or
something. So please Mom let me go outside.

Nancy

*   *   *

Tactful lesson

To: Mom
From: Terri
    You did not have to get mad at me you hurt my
feelings and you also made me very very sad.
So please do not do that again.
Good bye now.

With love,
Terri

*   *   *

Unconditional love

Mom,
  I love you.
        You settle fights,
        You give me love,
        You are a delight,
        You are my mom
  I love you!!!

                    Love,
                    Ginny

*   *   *

Expressing mixed feelings

Dear Mom,
  My tooth fell out!!! But I'm not happy because
Mary said "GROSS GET OUT OF HERE" and
Johnny said "GET OUT OF HERE FAGET," and
Jimmy said "I DON'T WANT TO SEE YOUR
FAGET TOOTH," I'm crying right now Ted's the
only one being nice to me!!! I'M SAD MIXED
WITH HAPPY Well anyway my tooth fell out!!!
But don't worry it's way in back so you can't see it.
                    Love, Suzy
P.S. TOOTH FAIRY!
also Mom, my tooth came out by me wiggling it
while I was in the bathroom. My tooth is on my
dresser BUT TELL THE TOOTH FAIRY NOT TO
TAKE IT!!!

* * *

Crime and punishment

Mom–Jean stole half of my smores bar!!! Jean
has to pay me 60¢ and give me some of her candy!!!
Jenny

* * *

Pinch hitter strikes out

Dear Mom–while you where gone Cathy swore and
she did not make pop-corn and she was being mean
and fighting with us an we did not do a thing and
while she was on the fone to her friend she tride to
be cool by being a bratt to me and sticking and
rubbing her feet on the TV and she made fun of me
AND she also said Qute: MOVE YOUR FAT
FACE!!!!!!!!!!!!!!

* * *

Prosecutor and judge

Mom,
Lou ate one or more Donuts and Eddie ate two or
more Donuts so none for them tomorrow.
Elsie

Getting mom's attention

> Oh Mother
> Dearest Please that is PRETTY Please would you get
> off of the phone because I have a show that I want to
> give you and granma and also before grandma goze
> to sleep and befor you go to sleep so please get off
> the phone!!!
>
> Love, Rebecca

*   *   *

Righteous anger

> Mom,
> Why in the HECK did you put my only pajamas
> and everything else in the wash jerk??!! Next time
> mind your own busnise.

*   *   *

Child's logic

> To: Dad.
> Thanks,
> For all the kisses you
> give me.
> (Even though
> i don't let you give them to me.)

Ask and you shall receive -
one way or another

Dear Mom,
　　I love you. You are the best mom in the world!
(in the whole wide world). Could I have a kiss and a
hug? I don't think you can but will you come
upstairs and watch T.V. with me? If you are going
to come upstairs with me then give me my kiss and
hug and come upstairs but if you are not then still
give me my kiss and hug and don't come upstairs.

Love,
Helen

　　P.S. I hope you can come upstairs with me!

*　　　　*　　　　*

Pride goeth before a fall

To: Bob
Bob, I am ready for bed good-night. This is my first
time putting up my hair by myself and I am very
excited mom doesn't even know I am putting up my
hair. I put up my hair better than Betsy and I can do
it even better! I didn't do it my best because I was
going super fast.
　　Well I have to go now so

Good-by
Love,
Jill

I'm ready for bed. It took me so long because I had
to redo a whole bunch.

*　　　　*　　　　*

TV sex education

Babies grow out of an egg in the Stomach and when they get done they come out your virginia and it stretches out and you have bladder problems. That's why you have to wear those pads that are like diapers. They show them on TV all the time and you can even jog in them.

The reason I know all that [facts of life] is because I have zits, black heads and pit stains.

*   *   *

Straight-forward logic

DIFFERENT DAY'S

Tomorrow is a different day.
Every day is different.
The only time
A day would be the same,
Is if the world went backwards!

Meg

*   *   *

Getting on mom's good side

Dear Mom, I am sorry for doing bad things and not doing what you say. My but is *really* red but it does not hurt so much. I will try not to say those bad things again!!!!!!!!

Love, I'm *sorry!!!*
Margie

P.S. I think tomorrow is brownies

78

Doubting diplomat

To: Mom ONLY!!!
I did this for you so maybe you would like me and if
your heart could be sweet and let me go outside. But
your heart could not be nice enough to let me go on
my bike so I won't ask too much!

Love,
Rachel

P.S. I made this weaving (the whole thing) while
you were gone.

*   *   *

Modern Cinderella

While You Were Gone
1.) Scrubbed each bathroom sink
2.) Did laundry
3.) Vacuum & dusted upstairs
4.) Vacuum & dusted middle floor
5.) Cleaned my room
6.) Straighten TV room, living room &
     Kitchen a hundred times
7.) Made lunch
8.) Made brownies
9.) Babysat

P.S. Charlie was hitting everyone with a stick thing
and him and Todd were imitating me because I told
them to shut up.

From
Angie (your summer girl)

*   *   *

Teenage touch

Read

Mom,.
    I'm going tomorrow morning at 6:00. Teri's mom will pick me up, we'll go over to Perkins then to school. There is just a slight problem. I need some moola. Maybe $5.00 if you kindly would put it on my dresser before you go to bed you would be most appreciated.

Your loving daughter,
Bridget

(same note)

Carrie,
    My loving sister, would you gracously spare some of your old rags since you probably got a new wardrobe. If you would kindly pick out something for me to wear I'll give you a piece of gum, next pack.
Pretty please with sugar, pulllleeeeeaaassee!

Love you,
Bridget

*   *   *

Santa's helper

Dear Santa,
   How come your so fat? You should go on a diet. If you see my Mom or Dad up ask them for their Stillmans or Enzymes diet. How's Mrs. Claus doing? So-long.

Love
Wendy

*   *   *

Frustrated child

Mad Mommy

Now do this Now do that
Don't say this Don't say that
Now your grounded
Now your not
If you be bad
I will get mad
So be good or I'll whip your but
      Dedicated to my Mad Mom

Sandy

Empty room

Take your stupid atlas - that gives you all the stinky
information You'll never want to know.
   & take your phony map
TAKE ALL THE THINGS YOU'VE EVER GIVEN
ME OUT OF THIS ROOM

Andy

Wrong color tag

Dear Mom, I don't like my LEVI'S because of
the stupid seems on the leg!!! and because their not
dark enough!!! and because they are
bellbottoms!!!!!!!

Love; Connie

Wail of a tale

To Mom–I know you do not like me. You only like
Bill, Jack, Joan, Peter, Mary and Jeff. You do not
like me. I dont mined at all because Dad likes me,
and Bill, Jack, Joan, Peter, Mary and Jeff Do not
like me. So I Do not care about you, because Dad
likes me and I like him. I know you like Bill, Jack,
Jean, Peter, Mary and Jeff but not me!!!!!!! And
Joan had to be a big pig and ate all my apple
cydre!!!!!!!!!!!!!!

Lisa

NOW I HOPE YOU THINK

      *   *   *

First-hand report

Mom, when you were gone Carol was making me
sick like I was going to ikspold!!!! She was doing it
all day!

Ben

      *   *   *

Future lawyer

THIS IS A FORMAL REQUEST TO:

JAMES E. AND CYNTHIA L. BROWN. I THE UNDERSIGNED DO FORMALLY REQUEST THAT THE CURFEW ENFORCED ON MYSELF AS OF AGE 13 BE REMOVED FOR THE REMAINDER OF MY LIFE AND A NEW ONE BE ENFORCED UNTIL FURTHER NOTICE. I HEREBY REQUEST THAT THIS CURFEW BE MAINTAINED AT 12:00 UNTIL FURTHER NOTICE FROM MYSELF.

THIS FORMAL REQUEST IS LEGALLY SIGNED BY,

SHARON ANNE BROWN
SHARON BROWN
(LEGAL DAUGHTER)

I HEREBY AGREE TO THIS NEW CURFEW OF 12:00 P.M.

X _____

X _____

Reaction to "Condemned Room" sign

HA-HA!

THAT SIGN was stupid! I don't think you get the message.. If I didn't share a room with Marsha you would be CRAZY about my room. I *wish* Marsha would not throw her things around the room! You get mad at me for no reason. You blame me for everyone else's faults. I am getting tired of all this "SWEETIEPIE" stuff about Marsha. If she would only pick up all her things. I get in trouble all the time for that.

Beth

*　　　*　　　*

Blue ribbon letter

Mom & Dad -

When I was born you had planted me. My vines grew into yours, yours grew into mine. You were part of me, I was a part of you. I've grown much bigger now, but even when you're an old vine, and I'm older too, we'll always be a part of each other.

I'll remember the times you took care of me, even when I was bad and grew those thorns. You would cut them off and teach me that was wrong. You've given me life and love, I couldn't ask for more.

Love -
Catherine

27

Children's Quotes

What Art Linkletter says is true: "Kids say the darndest things!" Not only are kids funny, they're often brilliant. Mothers should keep a notebook to record the choice comments, since children love to hear things about themselves when they get older.

HERE ARE SOME QUOTES FROM LITTLE BOYS ...

Child Guidance

When asked why he was such a good boy, a five-year-old commented, "My spirit tells me what to do!"

*   *   *

No Sweat

A youngster watching a soap opera with his Grandma, ignored his mom's pleas to get outside and swim on a hot day. Finally, coming out in his swimsuit he said, "My body couldn't hold the sweat anymore!"

*   *   *

Medical Art

The artist in one child came out in an unusual manner when he woke up ill. He said, "The colors of my body are all mixed up!"

*   *   *

Pleasant Dream

A six-year-old commented at breakfast one day, "I was dreaming I was kissing a beautiful girl—not like Lisa, [a school friend], but a *beautiful* girl, and I was 19!"

*   *   *

Broken Pumpkins

Seeing broken pumpkins in the street the morning after Halloween, one sensitive child observed them quietly for awhile, then said sadly to his mom as she drove the car, "Don't hit any of the dead pumpkins!"

*   *   *

Second Coming

Observing crocuses dying, a child commented, "The flowers are fainting!" His mom told him they were dying, and he philosophized, "Bury them so they'll rise again."

*   *   *

Sexism

A lesson that the news media might remember is that they're dealing with all ages. When a six-year-old heard the word "sexism" mentioned on TV he became angry. "Don't they know there are small children in the audience?"

*   *   *

Equal Opportunity

One small boy had been a professional model since birth. After two weeks of daily modeling in front of cameras and bright lights, he was tired and asked his mother, "Am I the *only* professional in this family?"

*   *   *

Cash On Delivery

When a young boy's mother finished cutting a neighbor's hair, the neighbor asked the boy how much she should pay his mother for the haircut. He said, "I don't know, but no checks, just cash!"

*   *   *

Young Doctor

One five-year-old said to his father who was bellowing, "Take an aspirin and go to bed!" Again to his father, "Don't let it come out of your mouth until you think!"

*   *   *

Wedding Plans

A six-year-old, after deciding he would get a TransAm first, before he found a wife, commented, "My bride will wear her helmet up the aisle!"

*   *   *

Smart Operator

A five-year-old greeted his mother one morning: "I'm so glad to see you awake and looking so bright!" Later, in exasperation, after repeatedly trying to get his mother's attention: "Mom, can I get you on the line, please?"

*   *   *

Indignant Protest

When coming in from his friend's house, a little boy saw his mom looking at him over her glasses. He said, "What are you looking at me for? Trying to see if I did something? Trying to see if I'm the culprit?"

*   *   *

Siberian Comfort

At the age of seven one little boy topped everyone. When his mother was upset he comforted her thus, "Don't think about it. Just think about marriage!"

*　　　　*　　　　*

Wrong Remedy

Another seven-year-old boy had a hard time controlling his mouth in school. He was so social. His mother suggested that when the teacher changed the seating, the boy sit by the girls to see if that would quiet him. To which the boy replied, "It's no use, I just *love* girls!"

*　　　　*　　　　*

Budding Poet

Observing the sun shining through the trees and a breeze blowing the leaves, a five-year-old said, "The leaves look like a light bulb trying to burn out."

*　　　　*　　　　*

Heavy Burden

One time when a five-year-old was modeling, his arms were propped straight out and clothes were piled on him until only his eyes showed. He quipped, "At least when they crucified Jesus he didn't have to wear all these clothes!"

*　　　　*　　　　*

Logical Explanation

On March 17th, when asked why he wasn't wearing green on St. Patrick's Day, another five-year-old said, "I'm no saint!"

* * *

Conscientious Practice

An 11-year-old boy learning to play the organ was questioned by his father, "Are you practicing the way Amadeus would?" To which the child replied, "You mean upside down and farting?"

* * *

No News Is Good News

Another eleven-year-old boy who was known to get into a little trouble occasionally, came home from school one day beaming as he said, "I had a *great* day today!" Mom asked, "What happened?" Said the child, "Nothing!"

* * *

NOW IT'S TIME TO HEAR FROM THE GIRLS...

Great Escape

One mother watched Phil Donahue one morning while hugging her pre-schooler on her lap. The child took all she could stand of Phil, then climbed off mom's lap, faced her, and with hands on hips said, "I would like to stay here and huggy-duggie-do, but I can't stand the TV. I'll be boring, and I'd rather be watching cartoons and be interesting!"

*　　　*　　　*

Literal Interpretation

An older brother listening to his three-year-old sister sing one day teased, "You should make a record, because you sing better than Barry Manilow." To which the tot replied, "I can't, because I don't have a hole in me."

*　　　*　　　*

Grandma Expert

A mother and her daughter were talking about grandmas. "Everything has a grandma. All the animals, people." Somehow the mother and daughter then got on the subject of acorn barnacles. Mom said, "An acorn barnacle puts its feet out and kicks food into its mouth." To which the pre-schooler replied, "I bet if it's a grandma, its leg shakes!"

*　　　*　　　*

Gives Up

Five-year-old girl to mom: "Remember, Mom, once I told you I was going to eat vegetables and all that good stuff?...I couldn't take it."

*　　　*　　　*

Resentful Child

Another little girl to mom: "You go out so much you're going to get in the habit. It's your hobby."

*　　　*　　　*

Concerned Child

Preschooler's famous return line to her mother after trying to run away: "Without me, who knows *what* would happen to you?"

*   *   *

Tiny Actress

A two-year-old, when she was upset with mom, "I just can't look at your cruel face. It's too much for me!"

*   *   *

Winning Through Intimidation

Another two-year-old's upset reply to mom: "I took a bite of shoestring candy, then I gave you a bite. I took a drink, then gave you a drink. After all I've done for you, you'd do *that* to me.

*   *   *

Mama Knows Best

A 14-year-old's observation: "Moms are like horoscopes that always come true."

*   *   *

Conclusion

Out of the mouths of babes quite regularly come gems.

V. Grade School Mothering

28

Keeping Your Cool

Two times of life come to mind when thinking about keeping your cool with younger children. The first is the toddler time when baby wants to get into everything. The second is when grade school and high school children start getting parents involved in car pools. Consider the toddler time first.

Keeping Cool With Toddlers

A child's awareness and initial independence may start at any early age, but it's generally the toddler time when baby hangs onto a table and begins to discover things. What a wonderland of treasures are awaiting that child's expanding curiosity. What wonderful fun and adventure! You'll have to put yourself into your baby's high-topped shoes to appreciate all the opportunities for learning that are within the reach of those tiny hands. How much fun it must be to touch glass, metal, paper, wood, flowers, and mud! How wonderful to touch and feel with four teeth! This is why your baby quickly outgrows a playpen.

When you figure a baby spends a great deal of time sleeping, eating, and getting changed, the time you spend following your baby around will be greatly reduced. Add to that the fact that baby loves to be by mom, and the problem seems simpler. When you're doing your work, for example, a playpen is wonderful. When you're working around the kitchen in safe, harmless, busy jobs, you'll have an opportunity to let your young adventurer explore.

Prepare a low cupboard for baby. When you go into the kitchen, sit baby in front of it and open the door. Make sure there are no breakables such as glass. However, pans, measuring spoons, jello molds, wooden spoons, and many other non-hazardous things can be in baby's cupboard. Also, the objects can be changed at different times. Pans that don't interest your baby can be put somewhere else, and a new toy can be substituted. Let your baby bang the pans around and experiment while you work. Once baby gets to know a special cupboard, the other cupboards will normally be left alone. That way you know by sight and sound where your baby is, so you can relax and keep your cool.

Keeping Cool With School Children

The second time it's difficult keeping your cool with children is when dealing with car pools. Car pools creep up on parents. First there's a car pool for religion classes. Then there are car pools for team sports. Add to those the car pools for music or dance lessons. The list is endless. If you have more than one child, the list multiplies by two, three, four, or more. With a large family, you'll think you're running a free taxi service! After a few years of car pools, parents either burn out or wise up. Let's hope they wise up *before* they burn out!

To be intelligent about this, parents have to set some priorities. Is a parent's time worth anything at all? If you've had your fair share of car pools throughout the school year, now, with summer coming, must you continue to devote your whole summer to car pools for one or more children? Is it important that your children be programmed every minute of every day, and that you also become programmed with car pools? Do your needs count for nothing?

There is a solution. Parents can tell each child, "I will drive only one car pool for each of you." That means the child doesn't play baseball, *and* soccer, *and* hockey, *and* football all summer. It means the child plays baseball, *or* soccer, *or* hockey, *or* football. Or, the child selects something close enough to *bike* to. Any boredom with the extra time should inspire creativity in your child. With fewer car pools, you may even discover that your own mind has been rationed a little extra time to think and create. Rejoice in your new time and remember, as your children grow older and become more independent, they won't be shocked when the world doesn't beat a path to their doors to entertain them.

29

Sports Versus Arts & Sciences Time

Most parents live in sports-oriented communities. Through their community parks, recreation departments, and fine schools, children may compete in almost any sport. Not only may children compete, but they're strongly urged by parents and peers to participate in at least one sport, and preferably many. Every minute of a child's spare time seems programmed toward excellence in sports. Not only in summer is this the case, but all year long. One mother of a "hockey child," whose husband also coached hockey, commented, "If a child isn't 'pro' caliber by the time he's eight years old, he's washed up in hockey in our community."

Children double up on sports. It's not unusual to see children on both baseball and soccer teams simultaneously, even though schedules conflict and one game or another must be skipped.

Mothers and fathers sitting on the sidelines are a sight to behold. Among others, a minister was once heard on the sidelines cursing his son at the top of his voice during an entire game. Coaches and refs are harangued as though they were high-paid professionals, rather than volunteers.

What does all this say to the children?"You *will* excel in sports!" "You *will* be on the traveling team." At the age of 10, "You *will* travel all over the country to play in tournaments like a professional." "You *will* make me proud." "You *will* be the star of the team."

Organized sports put too much pressure on kids. Sports are taken too seriously. They aren't much fun anymore. Increased costs of higher education and competition for scholarships are probably to blame for a lot of sports abuse. Many parents urge their kids to excel in sports so that the kids are offered college scholarships. Parents keep thinking about the big money earned by the pros. Yes, what about the pros? How few are the kids who get there, compared to the many who try!

When you add up all the hours spent in sports, including time in car pools, the amount is outrageously lopsided compared to the meager time spent reading, writing, or improving arts and sciences skills.

Most sports such as baseball, football, soccer, hockey, and basketball become purely passive spectator sports when a child grows up. Sports like tennis, golf, skiing and skating might be continued after working hours, but not to any major extent. Skills most needed out of school seem to get the least emphasis during school. Sports predominate.

Wouldn't it be wonderful if such subjects as reading, writing, and speaking could be given the same glory as sports? We all need to read, write, and speak throughout our lives, whether it be reading books, writing letters, preparing job applications, giving reports, filling out forms, paying taxes, making grocery lists, and on and on. Unfortunately, how little time is devoted to such activities in school, out of school, or during the summertime. Musical instrument lessons, for example, are often abandoned in the summer, even though that's the season a child has the most time to practice such lessons. Then parents complain they're in a car all summer, driving

101

sports players for a car pool, driving themselves to see games, or chauffeuring kids to some other organized activity. Parents soon begin looking forward to the day when sports are done, and they get a little time for themselves.

A few years ago, there were no organized park board or other summer teams as there are today. Children were forced to create their own sand-lot sports. A call went out in the neighborhood that some kind of game was being organized. Kids played in the otherwise quiet residential streets, school yards, or public parks. Usually a neighborhood street was good enough. Everyone played; no one watched. Everyone made the team. The ultimate reward was to hear your baseball peers say "heavy hitter," then move to the outfield when you came up to bat. If the weather was too hot to play, you didn't. No one remembered the score of a game or harangued a kid's mistakes.

Kids can create their own fun, given the chance. My own childhood summer was a wonderland. Although short in wintry Minnesota, it was full of happy memories. All of us kids were refreshed for the coming school year. Our uninhibited creativity was expressed in sports, exercise, reading, climbing trees, playing games, taking music lessons, being alone to dream, or joining with a gang of kids to play and share.

Kids today aren't allowed enough unprogrammed time. Parents seem afraid to let children alone for fear they'll become bored. Yet boredom in children is the springboard of creativity. When are children ever allowed to indulge their creativity.? Unless they have some time to themselves, when will they read? When will they ever appreciate free time for the gift it is? When young adults who are used to being programmed have free time after graduating from school and leaving home, they're at a loss as to what to do with themselves. They become restless and depressed. Many get into trouble.

Parents need to challenge their children's minds. They'll not always be around to tell their children what to do, or see that they're entertained. Children should have the opportunity while they're young, to learn how to make good use of spare time, so it becomes a lifetime habit.

30

What To Do About Music Lessons

How long parents hold out against the constant nagging of children to quit music lessons, seems to be the measure of how long a child actually takes them. An average might be about a year of a kid's badgering before parents throw in the towel and decide to quit knocking themselves out. Parents shouldn't expect their kids to eventually make a living with their music. Rather, it would be nice if children could play for their own enjoyment some day.

Unfortunately, the young years of grade school make adulthood appear to be a distant and unrealistic goal. Children don't want to practice music lessons. They demand freedom for enough leisure time, so they can nag us about what to do with it. The kicker is what happens when these same kids reach young adulthood. Soon music is everything, and musicians are admired. As young adults, children regret that they quit their music lessons. But do they get angry at themselves? Certainly not. They start fuming at mom or dad for allowing them to quit. *"Why* didn't you make me keep taking my lessons? I *would* have if you had *insisted."* Then parents have second thoughts about what really happened, and they start regretting their decisions, which they now regard as short-sighted.

Parents shouldn't do it! They should remind their children it's never too late to learn to play a musical instrument or take music lessons. Of course, the difference now is that the children, rather than their parents, will be paying for their instrument and lessons. Such news won't make the children very happy, but it takes the guilt from the parents and puts the challenge where it belongs. Also, if children start paying for their instrument and lessons, they'll treat them both with more reverence and appreciation.

The bottom line is this: any talent children can be encouraged to use and develop will grow and add to their self-esteem and sense of fulfillment, to say nothing about their own enjoyment. The secret is not to expect greatness in everything they try, but that they try to experience many of life's challenges. It's called, "becoming well-rounded."

Even if children only take lessons for a short time, they'll learn something. A little knowledge can add to their overall appreciation of music. By realizing how difficult it is to play an instrument, children grow in their admiration of those who do play well. They also listen with more intelligence and understanding. Consider music lessons as a good course in music appreciation, and be sure to *rent* the instrument rather than *buy* it!

31

Promoting Arts & Sciences

Every so often something wonderful happens to restore one's enthusiasm for the goodness in human nature. Recently, the PTA of a local elementary school organized, sponsored, and ran a festival to encourage children to take an interest in the arts and sciences. It was the first of what has become an annual event.

The festival has three evenings connected with it. First is *Motivation Night,* which is an evening when grade school students are motivated by professionals in acting, dancing, writing, speaking, music, comedy, and other arts as well as sciences. At that time, children are encouraged to register for individual events in which they choose to compete. After this first registration session, children are given several months to prepare their projects.

The second event is the *Fine Arts and Sciences Competition,* when individual children compete in the various activities before judges. Children present their projects or perform their selections, and professionals judge the projects or performances. Every child participating receives recognition in the form of a certificate acknowledging the child's participation and achievement. Every child, therefore, experiences success and a positive result.

The third session is *Awards Night,* when competitors are recognized and given their awards. First place winners present their project or performance again before peers and parents. First place winners were originally supposed to win $25 savings bonds, but on Awards Night, they were each awarded a ribbon, a certificate and a $50 savings bond. Second and third place winners were awarded ribbons and certificates, also.

Support for the competition was surprisingly strong, with only a few negative comments. For example, a couple of people wondered why second and third place winners got only ribbons and certificates without any savings bonds. Then something wonderful happened.

At the end of the *Awards Night,* parents of two girls approached the program chairman. The two girls had won six $50 savings bonds for a total of $300. Their talents were extraordinary, and now their parents wanted to thank the chairman for the unusual opportunity the festival competition had given them as a family.

The chairman soon learned what set that family apart. The unusual family not only decided together what events the girls would compete in, they also rehearsed and worked as a family to polish the girls' performances. The effort showed, so the awards came as no surprise to anyone. Also, on the evening before the competition, the family gathered together, and the parents told their children how much they had enjoyed the whole experience. They also told the girls they wished them luck, but that winning the bond would be second only to the great fun they had experienced as a family.

After the awards were presented, mother then said to the chairman, "instead of the $50 savings bonds for each event, couldn't we share the extra $25 with the second and third place winners?" Her husband and girls had agreed. What a pleasure it is to discover such a family and realize how much goodness there can be that we rarely hear about. Although the girls' work was their own, the competition was the opportunity for their family to have fun as a family group.

106

32

Helping With Homework

Some parents may be able to help their children with homework, but they're smart enough not to. It should be expected that children do their own homework without help. Start off right with your first child, and all of them will do their own homework. Only on rare occasions do parents need to help, and that might be, for example, with flash cards or interpreting subjective math problems. If children are in the habit of doing their own homework on time, they will. If they're in the habit of leaning on parents to do their homework, because parents encourage them to, they will.

Given the responsibility of doing their own work, most children will rise to the occasion. They usually realize that by third grade, the new math has left their parents far behind, so it's better to leave parents out of it. Kids don't want to end up having to teach parents!

During primary grades, homework shouldn't be necessary. Teachers and students have been together six hours, plus lunch time, and coming and going time. If that isn't enough of a day devoted to schoolwork, the educational system is wrong. When adults come home from a day at the office, for example, they're called work-a-holics if they bring more work home. Experts recognize the need for adults to relax and unwind. How much more do children need to "leave the work at the office!" Maybe adults began their work-a-holic behavior in grade school with homework.

When children miss a day of grade school, it seems that all the work they missed is made up in less than an hour. This leads one to suspect that all schoolwork may fit into less than a six-hour day. If a six-hour day is more than enough, and a child is experiencing learning difficulties, where better to solve such problems than in school? Occasional work may need to be done at home, (with stereo blasting?), but that shouldn't be overdone.

The parents' role of educating their children should be that of home-front supervisor. If a serious problem arises, teacher should notify parents immediately, so that teacher, parents, and child can work together to solve it. Otherwise, school should be a child's responsibility, not the responsibility of parents. By meeting and fulfilling their responsibility for schoolwork on their own, children are encouraged to grow in self-reliance, self-knowledge and self-esteem.

33

Evaluating Teachers, Tenure, And Discipline

The teacher crisis is serious in more than one respect. Teachers have been losing jobs because of declining birth rates; some schools have been forced to close; and surviving teaching staff has become much older due to tenure. Tenure is sacred. Teacher competency and quality yield to tenure. The result is that children, parents, and community pay the price of a deteriorating education system.

What's being done about the tenure problem? Virtually nothing under the present system. Only a teacher who does something outrageously bad or immoral may be brought before the School Board for a hearing and possible reprimand, but rarely is there any dismissal. The lazy, undedicated, incompetent teachers, including the ones who either vocally or silently insult, intimidate, humiliate, demoralize, or psychologically damage children, seem untouchable because of tenure. What has been done about such teachers? Nothing, they're still around. What about a personality conflict in kindergarten or other grades, where an unfit teacher makes a bad entry on a child's record? That record circulates from grade to grade, getting embellished every year, and can adversely affect the attitudes of future teachers toward that child. As usual, the child suffers.

One local school recently started a so-called "Assertive Discipline Program." Basically, it's supposed to encourage good behavior in children by recognizing and rewarding it. Unfortunately, most administrators and teachers don't really understand the concept. The result is that they use assertive discipline as a new kind of punishment device. Kids are given demerits for bad actions and suffer the consequences: cancellation of a movie or field trip, suspension of a popcorn party, denial of free time set aside for play. Problem is, who are the adults dealing out the punishments accountable to? No one.

Consider how the school administers Assertive Discipline. Children are given demerits for unacceptable behavior and rewards for good behavior. Only one demerit may be given at a time. After two or three demerits, rewards are taken away.

Yet, some teachers are giving children two or three demerits for simply looking at disturbances. That's not playing by the rules. The children are being treated unjustly.

Children have a strong sense of justice. There's no faster way to destroy a well-intended program than to install it without checks and balances. Students become alienated, they adopt negative attitudes toward education, and their futures are adversely affected. For such abused children, instead of an enjoyable experience, school becomes little more than a place where improperly employed adults establish lists of infringements to use as a basis for persecuting kids.

Assertive Discipline is simply the newest means that bad teachers use to inflict harsh punishment on children. This unfortunate program consists of various schemes used by teachers and other school employees to aggressively control children via oppressive punishments for various rules infractions. Thus, Assertive Discipline gives bad teachers an opportunity to become worse. When some good teachers were asked what they thought of the Assertive

110

Discipline Program, they said they really never chose to use the program, and simply ignored the principal's orders.

Bad feelings of children about their schools are created in other than classroom situations, especially where the Assertive Discipline Program is used in hallways, on playgrounds, and in lunchrooms. For example, teachers at one school were asked to grade children for behavior in the lunchroom. The average grade was D+. Not knowing about lunchroom behavior grading, parents were invited by their PTA to have "Lunch with the Bunch." Parents could pick any day, buy a lunch ticket, and eat lunch in the school lunchroom with their child. When they did, they were shocked.

Instead of a happy, relaxing time, lunch hour was severely strained. Students weren't allowed to speak while standing in endless, slow moving lines. Parents, however, began visiting with each other while standing in line with their children. Soon their children grew increasingly nervous. When asked what was the matter, the children said that if anyone got caught talking in the lunch line, the line would be stopped until the talking ceased.

When sitting at a table, mothers noticed that a grim-looking, unsmiling janitor, plus several other school staff members or "guards," had been posted around the lunch room, arms folded in front of themselves, eyes glaring and scouring the room. When the lunchroom cleared, the various "guards" walked up to the janitor and submitted lists of names of student offenders.

One mother commented that the lunchroom serving line moves so slowly, most of a child's lunchtime is spent waiting in the line. Also, children wanting only milk to go with their bag lunches have to wait in line with children who are waiting to buy lunch. The whole arrangement is insane. Children are being organized and set up to fail. As tables are cleared, children are moved and concentrated at other tables. Visiting mothers having "Lunch with the Bunch" had to move with their children more than once. Each of these moves meant picking up one's various lunch items and moving with them to another table. After several moves like that in the middle of eating, one realizes the insanity of such an arrangement.

The Assertive Discipline program is used in many schools. The negative attitudes it fosters are the same, no matter whether generated in lunchrooms or classrooms. Rather than looking for the good in children, teachers and staff personnel are encouraged to look for the bad. Such an approach ruins children and stifles learning. It has nothing to do with learning. It has to do with punishment.

Good teachers don't need bad discipline programs. Good teachers love children first of all; secondly, they love to teach. Children aren't fooled. They're quick to spot a phony. Children have a way of knowing when they're truly loved, and they usually return that love. When there's love, children can learn under almost any kind of adverse conditions.

Schools have many fine teachers.

PARENTS ONLY ASK THAT...

When a teacher is bored or tired;
Or when kids become bothersome;
Or when lesson plans aren't varied from year to year;
Or when everything is graded "C" for "Corrected" instead of being given a proper grade;
Or when a teacher races kids out the door each afternoon;
Or when teachers leave classes unattended for long periods of time;
Or when teachers embarrass kids in front of others or hold them up to ridicule;
Or when kids with a strong sense of justice don't like an unjust teacher anymore;
Or when a teacher is prejudiced against one sex or the other, or a particular race;
Or when unreasonable assignments are given to keep kids quiet for days, weeks, and months;
Or when a teacher loses a sense of justice and fair play;
It's time that the teacher moves into another career.

Many people are in the wrong career or get burned-out. In the business world, Burned-out people switch jobs, employers, or, if necessary, careers. In teaching, however, many good teachers get laid-off, while many bad teachers keep teaching because of a crazy tenure system. Unfortunately, the children, who are supposedly the beneficiaries of our system, are the big losers. Tenure has become a tragedy.

Parents should get active in their local schools. They must familiarize themselves with the system that controls their children's minds and bodies for so long a time every day, then act courageously to change it if necessary.

34

Reshaping Sex Education

Most schools now have sex education on a continuing basis throughout the entire grade school years. In our community it's known as the "Family Life Series." Whether it's a good series depends to a great extent on the teacher doing the instructing. An important question to ask is, if there were no continuing "Family Life" course, how would children learn about sex? Would TV be their teacher? Would love ever enter into their understanding of sex? Love doesn't get much more coverage in school than on TV, but at least it's some coverage.

At our house, sex education is dinner conversation. By that I mean when the meaty facts are discussed in fifth and sixth grades at school, that evening the new expert will announce at the dinner table, "We had sex education at school today!" From each end of the table, my husband and I will stop in mid-chew, stare at each other, and steel ourselves for the next hour and week.

With the younger children it's more fun. We have been through seven sex education discussions, with one to go for our youngest child. These discussions have become even more fun now, because older brothers and sisters around the table participate, too. My husband and I have learned a lot from them, and in recent years have acted more as moderators between age groups than bastions of authority. That is, we moderate whenever we get a chance to speak at all!

Kids never change. The day before these heady sex-oriented facts are given to them in school, kids are told there's to be no snickering during instruction. Naturally, most kids wear turtlenecks on the big day, so their snickering can be easily concealed. Boys and girls are seated together for some topics, then separated into different rooms for others.

In a child's younger years, with all the new awareness and education about sex, it seems logical to assume that sexual activity in the child's older years will be less of a problem. That's what parents are told. However, the fact of the matter is that sexual activity has become a much greater problem. Parents should re-assess their school's entire sex education program, and inject greater awareness of the need for love and the importance of one's responsibilities for consequences. Maybe parents are too clinical about sex. Maybe they aren't telling their children about the serious responsibilities that accompany sexual actions. Sexual activities do tend to be regarded separately from their primary purpose, which is the creation of life.

Children need to first understand what their responsibilities as parents will be. After that they can learn how to become parents. The school's sexual education program tells children from kindergarten through high school about reproduction in plants, animals, and humans. Rarely does it teach them about good parenting, love, devotion, sacrifice, hard times, good times, life.

In high school, time is spent discussing birth control methods, the signs and dangers of venereal diseases, and other such items. No parenting. Just clinical facts.

115

Recently a mother remarked that one of her daughters, who was a sophomore in college, called her up after 10:00 p.m. one night, frightened and weeping her sad tale. "One of my roommates has herpes and one has crabs!" Later, when feelings had settled down, an interesting fact surfaced. The woman's daughter said that herpes and other social diseases had been discussed in a matter-of-fact, clinical way during high school. What the daughter then remarked was, "They never told us about the terrible pain and suffering involved, the nightmare created psychologically for the sufferer, the depression, the permanent nature of the problem, and the terrible, long-term effects."

Maybe it's time people quit supporting sexual freedom. Maybe it's time parents insist that the family be put back into the picture and given the position of respect it deserves.

VI. Mothering Teens

35

Seventh Grade, Or Walking Into The Face Of The Cannon

Kids experience one of their first adolescent culture shocks when they begin seventh grade. Smaller elementary schools give way to larger junior highs, and junior highs are followed by a single, much larger, senior high school. Each school change a child makes signals the death of one kind of life, and the birth of a new one. It's not easy for any child. It's especially not easy for a beginning seventh grader.

After graduating from grade school and experiencing a major ego trip as a member of the top grade there, the new seventh grader now ranks at the bottom of the ladder in junior high. Having watched their sixth grader prance in grandiose fashion for the past year, parents are surprised when their self-assured child turns into a shy, embarrassed, somewhat fearful seventh grader.

119

God only knows how much seventh graders could use some humility for a change, but parents don't like to see their child suffer. If the child has changed from a private school to a public school, the transition can be harder for that child than for most. If the change is from one public school to another, the transition may be somewhat easier. Parents should remember, however, that even the smoothest transition from either a private or public school is difficult.

So what can parents do? They can again start showing their child some love. Parents, of course, have always loved their child. But remember, they've been watching their sixth grader prancing in grandiose fashion for the past year! Also, they've taken a back seat to their child's peer group. Naturally, they're filled with a few "serves 'em rights." Maybe they've even slacked off a little in showing enough love for their heady sixth grader. Seventh grade is the time for parents to start showing their love again for their newly humbled child.

About midway through seventh grade, kids begin feeling their oats once again, and may even revert back to their cocky prancing. When the children are just beginning seventh grade, however, parents should love them when no one else will, give comfort when needed, boost egos, and in general, remind them of their unique gifts which they may have temporarily forgotten. The beginning of seventh grade and junior high school is the parents' opportunity to take their frightened child by the hand once more, and carefully help that child enter another unknown, scary time of life. Mom and dad did it for kindergarten; they can do it again at the start of junior high, then senior high, and even college.

36

Coping With Peer Groups

"Peer group pressure" is a mysterious, even threatening group of words that can spell big trouble for parents. When children are young, they adore their parents. Mom and dad can do no wrong, know all things, and never make mistakes. Whatever mom and dad say or do is perfect. So what happens when kids get to junior high and become teenagers? Almost overnight, it seems, parents have fallen from the high pedestal on which their children had placed them. Parents have now become an embarrassment to their children. Mom and dad can do no right, know nothing, and always make mistakes. Whatever mom and dad say and do now is wrong.

Be assured, the world has not changed overnight. Parents have not been suddenly transformed. Prince Charming didn't get turned into a frog. The good fairy godmother didn't become a wicked witch.

Mother and dad didn't suddenly become senile. Parents are merely witnessing another kind of birth in their child, the birth of a teenager.

When a teenager is born into the new kind of life, the old kind is completely discarded, even denied. Yes, denied, not merely ignored. Parents, who were relied on and trusted for good advice, are now silenced. For mom or dad to say anything in public is to embarrass their teenager into panic and rigidness. In fact, for parents to even *recognize* their teenager in public is a "faux pas." Teens won't allow parents to exist as anybody but servants. With newborn teenagers around, parents should plan to hibernate their mouths for the next 3-6 years!

The "peer group" is the new life teenagers are born into. Even though a full school day has been spent with the peer group, before a teenager gets home after school, the telephone will have rung four or five times. Hour long phone conversations become common. Noise-blasting stereos, designer jeans, dirty tennis shoes, "zit" cream, outrageous behavior, big appetites and a passion for chocolate and gum are parts of the emerging teenager.

Fear not, teen life too shall pass. But before it does, a parent's ego will be operated on and dissected into oblivion. Parents will have to find a sympathetic peer group of their own to salvage whatever shred of sanity they have left. They should avoid adored mothers of young children! Rather, they should mingle with badgered moms and dads of other teens, including those who have already survived the teen years of children, and who can give encouragement and assurance that a teenager's adolescence will eventually pass.

Fortunately for some parents, their children emerge from adolescence in good condition. However, the peer group is still very much a part of their teen children's years, and the children still judge themselves by the standards of their peers. They see themselves either measuring up, or not measuring up. Rejection can be dangerous, but it's heartening to know that peer groups often mellow, and ripen into true and lasting friendships.

After older teenagers have gone away to college for awhile, or moved out of the house to be near work, they begin to notice that their parents are becoming smarter and more knowing. These teenagers don't accuse parents of making so many mistakes. They may even allow their parents to talk once in awhile, possibly in public.

When a grown child comes back home to visit, the metamorphosis in that child's thinking is an inspiration. Morale and self-respect of parents blossom anew as their child suddenly discovers how much parents have learned, and how wise they've now become since the child left home. Also, new peer groups of college or work friends replace the giddy high school peer group, and their common bond of poverty becomes a leveler.

It's usually during the trying teen years that parents, somewhat smilingly and mischievously, wish their teenagers could have children of their own someday, *in the teenager's own image and likeness.* Do you suppose our parents wished that for us?

37

Putting Up With The Pecking Order

Volumes have been written on a child's order of birth into a family. That's family "pecking order." Another kind of pecking order is when children play. Each neighborhood has its own pecking order, very much like that of a family.

Neighborhood children gather in groups. Certain children play with certain children. If some kind of game is being formed by older children and various warm bodies are needed, younger children might get an exciting invitation to join the game. Why is it that children play nicely when there's an even number for playing, but then invariably start fighting when there's an odd number? Why does one grade level in grade school make such a difference? The answer is pecking order.

Some neighborhood kids may bully certain children who are lower down in the pecking order. The cruelty that these tormented children are forced to endure can be devastating. It may leave long-range emotional scars and bad memories. What cruel lessons about life these tormented children are forced to learn at such a young age, through no fault of their own. One bully is all it takes. Unless someone stands up to that bully, no one will prevent the more vicious and often criminal behavior that follows.

It usually does no good to talk to parents of a bully. The bully has probably learned abusive behavior at home. The bully's parents may be meek and brow-beaten by the child, abusive and bullies themselves, or simply indifferent to whatever their child does. If nobody acts to correct the situation, everyone will have to wait for a bully to grow older and leave home. Not a happy prospect for the rest of the neighborhood kids. The other choice is to move to another neighborhood. The problem with that is, parents may find another bully.

As soon as parents get pecking order problems cleaned up, they'll make their neighborhood a happier place, and set a good example for their children. It's essential parents try to do this, because their neighborhood is an extended family. Children are first nestled in the family. If they're loved and nurtured there, they have a chance for a good beginning. If we can all live in peace in our families, in our neighborhoods, and in our communities, maybe then we'll be able to achieve world peace.

There has to be continuing love and support outside the home, too, if all children are to grow and develop well. Those nurtured by hate, indifference, or rejection, have to be changed somehow. Their difficulties probably began negatively at home, and may have to be changed there. But if not, maybe the neighborhood can help. Sometimes wickedness in someone else's child can't be readily changed. It's too deeply ingrained. Parents should teach their children to simply walk away from such troublesome children if change for the better seems hopeless.

Being alert to bad situations can have a positive result. The negative example of the bad situation teaches others how not to live and what behavior not to imitate.

An understanding of pecking order begins with a family's roots. It looks at how children were treated in their family and neighborhood. How children were treated themselves is how they'll usually treat others. Children who have been shown fairness and kindness are usually fair and kind. Sometimes, those who have been treated unfairly and unkindly learn compassion, rather than how to be unfair and unkind. Those who continue to be unfair and unkind, however, especially those who get away with it, will probably grow in their wickedness.

38

Understanding Truancy Problems

While teaching a special, once-a-week evening class to seventh graders, a teacher ran across a truancy problem. There was a boy who seemed to be doing fine, appeared to be enjoying the class, but then didn't show up for a few weeks.

When discussing the matter with the boy's mom, the teacher noticed that she seemed disturbed. Her son was having a rough time with his classmates, she said. They made fun of him. Johnny (not his real name) said he was being ridiculed. That's why he didn't want to come to the class anymore.

The teacher asked Johnny's mom to send him to class once more, so the teacher could have a chance to work on the problem. The teacher thought it was a strange problem because she had never noticed any kind of negative behavior towards Johnny by his classmates. The teacher's daughter and a very popular neighbor boy were in the class. When asked privately if they were aware of any ridiculing of Johnny, both said no; Johnny was quiet, and none of the kids had ridiculed him.

The teacher prepared a special lesson on the importance of friendship. Since the class had been rotating its location weekly, it happened that the next meeting was at Johnny's house.

During the entire lesson, the class was most attentive. Johnny's dad had been invited to sit in on the class, as was the custom for host parents. He sat quietly and never said a word. After the class, when the students had left, the teacher asked Johnny's dad what he thought of the lesson. Sarcastically, he said the students probably weren't even listening. He then began verbally assaulting the teacher, and bad-mouthing the rest of the class. He said Johnny wouldn't be coming to the class anymore, and Johnny never came again. However, Johnny wanted to come.

It soon became obvious to everyone that Johnny's problem wasn't with his classmates and their lack of friendliness. It was with his father. When calling about Johnny the next day, his teacher said she began to understand the sadness in Johnny's mother's voice. The teacher let Johnny's mother know that the class was sorry to lose Johnny, but that she and Johnny's classmates did try to make him happy.

Johnny's teacher and classmates were concerned, because Johnny wasn't being ridiculed by his classmates at all. He was really being ridiculed by his father. Not all truancy problems are a child's fault. A happy child doesn't need to be truant. A troubled child needs a sympathetic friend; either a parent or someone else who will listen.

39

What To Do When Kids Think They're Smarter Than Mom

Children suddenly become brilliant somewhere on their way to adulthood. At least they *think* they've become brilliant. Somewhere around sixth grade, again at junior high, and finally in eleventh or twelfth grade, kids seem to get impressed by their own wisdom. What it boils down to is this: when they get along with their parents, children figure it's because they're smarter than the parents. So let them be. If parents get a few minutes' peace it's worth it.

Sometimes a junior-higher attempts to negotiate permission to go on overnights. Perhaps parents are told it's someone's birthday; or the hostess' mother loves their daughter and misses her; or the host family is going on vacation or moving away, and this is the one last party; or, something special is going on early next morning, like a school group breakfast. If parents are against overnights, as many are, they may want to do some cautious checking first before allowing their child to attend.

Sixth graders and those younger figure all they have to say is they're going to "play at the park," or "go on a bike ride," or "jog." Seems at this level they begin to assert a little independence. When they're a bit older, however, and a girl friend calls, or vice versa, we're not to guess they're "going" together. Formal sex education in grade school has been completed, and pre-teen kids now think they're experts, at least until boys hear the word "menstruation" on TV and have to ask mom what it means. Teenage kids develop the weird logic that has them call black, white, and white, black. They regard their parents as incredibly stupid if they fail to appreciate such logic.

The biggest challenge is in senior high school. How can parents endure such brilliance? Children twist parents around their fingers, and snooker them with creative excuses. Parents are supposed to be completely taken in by a teenager's extraordinary brilliance on almost every subject. Senior high schoolers regard themselves as the repository of all knowledge.

As one stupid parent to another, I say go with it! When children want something, let them butter you up. It may be their last kind word to you for the week. In fact, if parents refuse, it *will* be their last kind words for the week starting right that second. When children want a favor, parents may as well take advantage of the situation and extort an agreement that the kids will do a load of wash first. Or, give them their night out if they'll babysit for you a night.

You get the drift? It's kind of like two lawyers trying a case. The ultimate goal is which one will snooker the judge. It's no different in business, school, or where it really counts with a teen, right at home. The good part is, teenagers aren't smart enough to be subtle. Play your cards right, and you can be the snookerer rather than the snookered!

40

Overcoming Embarrassing Oversights

Writing about this incident is an exercise in humility. If it had happened to anyone else, I wouldn't have believed it. Unfortunately, it happened to me, so I know it's true.

We have eight children, so we don't usually go out to restaurants. An inexpensive fast-food treat is what we usually get when we do go out. One weekend, however, we decided to go to a special restaurant about a mile from home.

When we arrived at the restaurant, there were so many of us we needed two separate tables next to each other. Our teenagers like to sit together at one table, so my husband and I sat with our younger children at another. We all enjoyed a great meal. Afterwards, our children stopped to wash their hands.

Whenever we're all in the car, I always count heads before going. This time I must have counted one head twice, because I thought we had everybody. Unfortunately, we didn't. After we arrived home, we quickly scattered throughout the house. Soon, one of the kids was looking for her ten-year-old sister, but couldn't find her. She asked me where she was. I said I didn't know, but started looking for her, too. No luck. We all started looking. Suddenly, one of our boys said he couldn't remember seeing his sister in the car when we drove home from the restaurant.

My husband rushed out of the house, jumped into the car, and drove back to the restaurant. He looked around, checked the restroom, asked questions, but couldn't find our lost daughter. He took an alternate route on the way home from the restaurant, and, half-way home, found her walking and fuming mad (this girl doesn't have red hair for nothing).

My husband and I got the tongue-lashing of our lives, and it was well deserved, I might add. Thankfully, the restaurant was close enough to our home so that our daughter could have easily walked the rest of the distance herself if my husband hadn't met her half-way.

My husband and I are no longer surprised when we hear on the news about parents who leave a kid in a restroom on a long trip, for example, then have to return 100 miles or more to retrieve the child. It can easily happen.

One bit of good came from this bad experience. When we go anywhere, the children are the first ones in the car!

41

Teaching Children To Save

A recent study of a wealthy suburban high school graduating class revealed these statistics: 71% of all seniors work at part-time jobs; 3% work over 25 hours a week. In middle and lower income schools, therefore, percentages are probably higher. The conclusion seems to be that most high school students have part time jobs.

What do working students do with their money? That's an important question. Some have a revolving charge account at the local clothing store that seems to have no limit; some eat their way through each paycheck; and some spend it all on entertaining themselves.

Where do parents fit into all this? As in other matters, they serve as their children's guide and example. Parents should encourage their children to open a savings account where savings can receive maximum interest. Also, it's important that parents take time to assist their children in understanding and anticipating future financial needs. Parents should even help children construct a budget and work out a sound savings program. They ought to encourage their children to save a portion of each paycheck. Occasionally, children will need money for a special event, special clothes, or for some emergency. Usually, however, children should save a consistent and substantial amount out of each paycheck. That way they can help pay for a college education or finance essential future needs without going into debt.

Parents do children a disservice when they allow them to shift for themselves. Whether it's money matters, discipline, work habits, or leisure activities, children need guidance and supervision. That's how they learn. Parents who give no guidance, or aren't interested in supervision, don't do their children any favors.

Parents are children's first and principal teachers, and children rely on their parents. Children will be on their own soon enough. They'll have to trust their own judgment, completely manage themselves, and make good use of their time and money. For these reasons, parents need to give their children the strongest foundation.

42

Importance Of Being Alert

One summer our family vacationed at a lake with a few relatives. This was one of the very few vacations we ever had. My husband and I stayed with our children in a rented cabin on one side of the lake. Several cabins on the other side of the lake were owned by my sister's husband's family. We were all having a wonderful time the first day until my sister broke her leg water skiing. That put her in a plaster cast and confined her to her cabin for the remaining two weeks of her vacation, plus several weeks after that.

While we were visiting my sister one day, our older boys went fishing. They were only about a city block away, so our three younger children were placed in their care. Unfortunately, the older boys left later with their cousin to get something to eat, but they didn't take our younger children along. When the older boys came back, the younger children were gone. Frantically the older boys called and looked for the missing children, but with no results. Then they came to my sister's cabin to see if our younger kids had showed up. No kids! That's when we got involved, and the search really began in earnest. We immediately drove back to our cabin on the other side of the lake, but our children weren't there either.

Hours passed. Police in the nearby town were notified, as well as passing CB'ers. If our lost children were on the main road and not drowned in the lake, we were sure they would be found.

The wife of my sister's brother-in-law finally spotted our lost children on the main road. She had looked down that road a dozen times before, but at those times the children had been taking a shortcut through fields and couldn't be seen. We were greatly relieved and thankful when the children were finally found. Soon we got down to the nuts and bolts as to how this all happened. It was extreme thoughtlessness on the part of all the children. We reasoned with them that if thought*less*ness caused all this trouble, then thought*ful*ness seemed the proper restitution. They were asked to think of a thoughtful task to perform each day for the rest of their vacation, then advise me what it was they would be doing.

One boy decided to visit his injured aunt each day for an hour and cheer her up, since with a broken leg and full cast her existence was bleak. None of the children were allowed to tell anyone that their thoughtful deed was restitution for their thoughtlessness. To this day, the children remember the lesson they learned, and our rare lake vacation, though troubled, remains a happy experience.

43

Knowing Children's Whereabouts

Quiet kids require their mother's and father's watchful eyes. This is especially important when such kids are teenagers. One of our boys is very quiet. He has a room on a lower level of our house and keeps pretty much to himself. During his early high school years, his weekend curfew was 11:00 p.m. He never argued about that curfew. In fact, he very seldom ever went out. At least that's what we thought.

There's a backyard stairwell door leading into our boy's room. At the bottom of the stairwell there's a drain that sometimes fills with water in heavy rains. When that happens, water floods under the door and into his room. We keep an eye on that drain in a heavy rain, so we can pump it out before the water gets too high.

One night we had a terrible downpour after our quiet teenage son had turned in early to study. I went down and knocked on his door, then asked him to check the drain. No answer. I repeated my request. No answer. I checked the door. It was locked. He must be asleep, I thought. The next five minutes would have waked the dead! No answer. Finally my husband went out into the pouring rain and walked around to the back of the house, so that he could get into the room from the outside. When at last my husband got into the room, our suspicions were confirmed. No son! He had gone out.

My husband got to the stairwell drain and siphoned it out in the nick of time to prevent flooding. While he was doing that, a devious plan was brewing in my mind. The hours passed. The bewitching curfew hour passed. No son. I went into my room and got ready for bed. Then I went downstairs to the prodigal's room, turned off the lights, and crawled into his bed.

Time marched on. One o'clock came and went. Finally, I heard a noise. Slowly the doorknob turned. Quietly, oh so quietly, the culprit came into his room and hung up his jacket. Quietly, oh so quietly, he tiptoed to his bed and SAW HIS MOTHER SMILING SWEETLY UP AT HIM!

44

Pros And Cons Of Spring Breaks

There's a new development in family life. It consists of parents whose children have traveled to more places in a few short years than their mother and father or grandparents have in a lifetime. Young people today are the most traveled of any people the world has ever produced. Our Planet Earth has truly become a small, small world.

Do you remember when our Spring Break approached? It was a school vacation time when we used to have one big wish, "Let's hope it doesn't snow or rain!" Nobody wanted to be cooped up in the house—mom or kids—for one or two long weeks. Today the big wish has a new twist: "Let's hope there isn't a revolution in that country;" or, "Is the rate of exchange favorable?" Or, "Hope the plane doesn't get hijacked!" No more the yesteryear worries about the weather in Florida, or whether pot, sex, and hard drugs are part of the concerts. A new era of world travel has arrived.

When parents were young they used to wish they could travel the world before they got too old to enjoy it. Now older kids wonder how they'll top their previous year's tour.

There are pros and cons about children traveling, but one thing is certain: the world is getting smaller. One great benefit could come from it: a new love and understanding among people of all nations, all races and all religions. How wonderful if this could happen, instead of the can-you-top-this-trip attitude.

Spring Break for our children might lead to the fulfillment of the hope of the world for peace and understanding. On the other hand, parents should guard against too much too soon. If kids have done it all by the time they're 25, will settling down be a settling downer?

45

Preserving The Family Car

No book on surviving motherhood could be complete without a chapter on the family car. When they have a teenage driver, parents soon understand why automobile insurance rates for such drivers are high. Explaining a new dent in the family car is an opportunity for a teenager's most creative storytelling and best acting performance. It doesn't matter that parents have driven family cars for decades without mishaps, or at least since *they* were teenagers. When the family car is driven by a teenager, accidents go looking for your car so they can happen.

The most popular accident excuse seems to center around parking lots, any kind of parking lot. No matter that for thirty years parents have been going to the same shopping centers, discount stores, fast food restaurants or filling stations without getting the slightest scratch or dent. When Old Betsy is let loose with a teenage driver, however, other cars seem to seek it out and bump it as it innocently sits unattended in the same parking lot it's been to without mishap hundreds of times before. That's only excuse number one.

When kids figure that excuse number one has been worked enough, and the family car is sufficiently well-pocked by parking lots, their ideas get more creative. One of the most creative but unlikely excuses heard recently was that a motorcycle rear-ended the family car, tearing away its bumper while the car was at a stop light. The unharmed cyclist was said to have then sped off into the night leaving the shocked teen so surprised she didn't think to get the cyclist's name or license number.

Another popular alibi is that the family car was parked at a curb while the teenager attended a meeting. Then another car backed into it and sped off, leaving no name or insurance information. The list of excuses grows. What about the teenager backing out of a parking space with the front door open, so that it gets crumpled by the bumper edge of a nearby car? Occasionally, kids have no excuse, such as when they hurriedly attempt to back out of the driveway at high speed, then crash into their parent's car parked behind the car the teenager is driving.

Parents hear so many creative excuses over the years that it seems their kids could become great fiction writers. However, when a car accident is a complete "total," with repairs beyond the body shop's ability, parents really have to take their hats off to the kids. One daughter couldn't phone her parents and tell them for four hours after a "total," because she said she was in "shock." The shock didn't come from any physical injury, however. It came, rather, from the fact that this child had the accident three days after she got a carefully reconditioned car, which was to be driven only to work and back. The shock came when she realized she had to explain to her parents how she and her roommate had the accident in another city, some fifteen miles away from her workplace, on her day off.

Any logical parent suffering through a child's teen years will come to one conclusion. Don't buy a new car for yourself, or even a newer car, until you're RID OF ALL YOUR TEENAGERS! Now I said logical parent. Can you believe my trusting husband wants to "upgrade" us and trade our two battered warriors for one newer car, when we have three more teenage drivers coming? Strange things can happen to men during the years of male menopause. That must be the explanation for my husband's lapse of sanity. A new car with teenage drivers? You're kidding.

VII. Emotions And Mothering

46

Setting A Good Example

Preach to your kids for years and years, tell them how to behave, and maybe you might get through to them. Be a good example, however, and they'll never forget the lesson. Why are all life's important lessons so simple? If you want good children, be a good parent. If you want honest children, be an honest parent. If you want loving children, be a loving parent. For example, it doesn't do any good if you tell your child about the evils of cigarette smoking or not to smoke, if you're a smoker yourself. It doesn't do your children any good to hear you tell about corruption on the church council or school board. You yourself should run for election to the council or board and try to change the situation. It doesn't do your children any good to hear you complaining about your community and your country. You yourself should set a good example of service and initiative by working to improve your community and country.

Nothing takes the place of good example, though we sometimes wish there was an easier substitute. How much easier it would be for parents if their children simply did as parents "said" instead of as parents "do." Parents can speak to their children about the standards of moral behavior expected. They can tell children what kind of behavior is required. But unless children see from example that their parents live by those morals, their parents' words are empty.

If parents view immoral TV shows and movies, or, if parents don't switch channels and protest such shows to sponsors, children will get a double-standard message: one rule for them; no rule for parents. Parents should realize that double standards are recognized by children.

Consider those fathers and mothers who won't tolerate bad language from their children, but who, when throwing a fit of temper, use the vilest and most vulgar language themselves. Such a double standard is outrageous.

There are parents who teach their children never to lie. Then these parents make glowing promises to their children, but never keep their promises. What must the children think?

What about the father and mother who brag about their children to all their friends, yet never support their children at home?

The examples of double standards are endless. Parents are all guilty of setting a bad example at one time or another. That's because they're human, and failure is part of everyone's life. Yet, because parents fail doesn't mean they should give up. A good example children must see is their parents picking themselves up after failing, then trying again a little harder until they succeed.

47

Controlling Anger; Forgiving Mistakes

"...and forgive us our trespasses as we forgive those who trespass against us." That's a powerful request people are asking of their Creator. Do they really understand or even think about what they're saying, or are those words simply prayed by rote? Forgive "seventy times seven?" And what about the Bible verse that says if we're coming to the altar and remember that someone has a grievance against us, we must leave our gift at the altar and go and be reconciled first with the person who has the grievance. Or, in another verse, if we're angry at our friend, we're "in danger of the judgment." The thrust of such messages is all too clear, painfully clear. The words are simple and uncomplicated. What's even more beautiful is the fact that they contain so much common sense.

Nowhere does the Bible seem to condemn anyone for being angry. Anger is one of the body's safety valves. Get angry, express it if you must, then forgive or be forgiven and get on with daily living.

Christ angrily threw money-changers out of the Holy Temple. We don't hear about it again, or whether it may have happened another time, so He must have forgiven them, and maybe they repented and changed their ways.

Ever feel like throwing a kid out? Ever do it? Ever get so angry you broke out in tears? Ever get frustrated with your child's sassy mouth, sloppy ways, weird friends, and lack of consideration? Ever tell your child about it in no uncertain terms? That's life! Motherhood and fatherhood isn't easy. Even the most gracious parents can get angry, or feel frustrated and helpless at times.

The most important thing parents can teach children about anger is that everyone gets angry. It's not the end of the world. The anger will pass. In fact, it's preferable that we express our anger to the cause of it, rather than let it build up inside and become like a festering cancer. People who repress and nurture anger are people who hold grudges and lose all capability of forgiveness. They either end up judging everyone (and we're told we shouldn't judge anyone), or else they end up with ulcers and other problems that destroy their own health.

It's good to have a few guidelines and affirmations of love established before anger develops. In our family, we've talked about the fact that even if we get angry with each other, we still love each other. When my ten-year-old girl got angry with me one day, I didn't try to stop her feelings. Rather, when she sheepishly came up to me later and said, "I suppose you don't like me anymore," I said, "I knew you loved me, but were just angry with me. And I'll always love you, even if I get angry with you."

When the offending person gets over being angry, simply forgive and forget. None of this silent treatment for days without end. It magnifies a mistake far more than it deserves.

Remember the friends of Jesus who were forgiven? Tax collectors, those possessed by devils, prostitutes, even a thief! Jesus of Nazareth forgave and befriended the wretched of the world, saying it was no challenge to have only good people as friends. That's too easy.

Parents need to help their children find the right balance. It's OK to feel angry, it's OK to express that anger, and it's OK to ask for forgiveness. Most of all, it's blessed to forgive.

48

Eliminating Jealousy

People have a knack for getting themselves into trouble. Trouble isn't limited to family, school, church, work or any other special category or time in one's life. Trouble is universal, and problems cross all social, political, and family barriers. If people were tuned in, they could see a pattern of trouble forming. The pattern isn't a pretty picture.

When people think back over problems they've experienced, they'll usually find jealousy as a frequent cause. Consider the child who is bullied on the school playground. Who caused it and why? How about the alienated parent, hostile neighbor, or lost friend? What caused the problems with them? Frequently, jealousy is the cause.

Family arguments often begin because someone isn't happy with the family income, usually in comparison to someone else's. Also, children with little talent cruelly persecute talented children, seemingly in direct proportion to a talented child's skills. The reason is jealousy. It happens among students, between brothers and sisters, with nearly everyone. Jealousy also occurs on a larger scale between countries. It corrupts leaders as well as followers. It's found in churches among members and clergy. It's found in schools among teachers. It's found in the business world among workers and executives. It's in the arts, sciences, government, everywhere.

It happened once, 2,000 years ago, in just one-week's time, that a man was lauded as a king one day, then exactly one week later he was crucified by the same crowd. Jealousy knows no bounds. It feeds on itself and spreads like cancer.

Maybe kids need some kind of hero to imitate, someone they can admire, rather than envy. Are their parents good examples? Children follow their parents' example, consciously and unconsciously, good or bad. It's up to parents to set a good example by eliminating jealousy.

49

Handling Rejection

Some people face more rejection than others because of their jobs. Radio announcers, TV personalities, models, actors, musicians, artists, singers, comedians, all have to live with rejection. Most people in the performing art professions face rejection.

For example, children who are professional actors, actresses, and advertising models are often exposed to rejection. They go to many auditions, but often fail to get the job. They're lucky though, because in the professional performing environment, children are taught at a very early age to be objective about rejection. It's nothing personal. A photographer, director, or client is just looking for a different face, voice, hair color, or any of a number of other special characteristics. A child rejected for one job may be selected for another job. Rejection is a routine matter. So should it be with school, sports, and other activities.

Parents should help their children learn how to handle rejection as routinely and objectively as children in modeling do. The lucky children who learn how to handle rejection are able to by-pass brooding and get on with life. Also, rejection in later years doesn't bother those children either.

Most children never have the opportunity to share their rejection with their parents the way that children in the professional performing arts do. Rejection for most children occurs on the school playground, in the classroom, or in the neighborhood. Parents rarely hear about it, or become aware of the need to give extra support to their child. However, if a child is loved by parents and is secure, life's occasional rejections won't be overwhelming or insurmountable. The well loved child is usually able to survive rejection on the school playground.

Are parents aware of the cruelty that may occur on their child's school playground? Are they aware of the obscene language? Are they aware of the many forms of rejection their child faces in school? Kids are imitating the bad behavior of someone somewhere. Maybe they're learning about rejection, insecurity, and bad language on the school playground, or maybe they're learning it at home.

Children are like freshly washed blackboards when they're born. Their slate is completely clean, not a mark on it. Then, as life writes on it, the slate becomes cluttered with good and bad experiences. Try as they may, some kids never seem to be able to wipe that slate clean again. Their lives are permanently marred. That's why parents should be concerned about what gets written on their children's slate. Also, they should teach their children to be concerned about what gets recorded on the slate.

Love, love, love! Will parents ever realize the power of love? Love is so powerful, it can help overcome any kind of rejection. It's mom's and dad's responsibility to be loving and to help their children understand how different human beings can be from each other. By their example, parents can teach kids that differences are to be expected. People don't reject someone because they don't like that person's skin color, religion, or economic status. However, people can and should reject bad behavior, and learn to avoid it. Kids, like anyone else, are going to meet people they don't like. They're going to have school teachers they don't care for. Also, not all people are going to like kids. Everyone's different. Each can be annoying to someone. Parents should teach their children to try to be nice to everyone. Good manners make a person nice to know.

Speaking about being nice to people and handling rejection reminds me of two conversations one of my children had with me. The conversations had to do with a rejection I experienced. I'm in the habit of singing along with the music I hear from the stereo. One day, I was happily singing along with music when one of my teenage boys said to me firmly, "I'd *like* to hear the *record.*" After that, whenever that boy was around, I was careful not to sing anymore. About a year later, he was talking with me and was concerned about my happiness. When I looked puzzled he said, "You never sing anymore." God help me, it's the truth!

50

Sharing Unemployment With Children

It seems that almost all families, at one time or another, experience unemployment. Our family's first such experience came shortly after my husband entered the business world, after changing from a teaching career. We had three children, no savings, a big mortgage, and car payments. That early bout with unemployment was followed by several others over the years. All the companies my husband worked for had mass layoffs during periods of economic recession. Each time he was thrown into a difficult job arena to compete for a shrinking number of jobs with thousands of other talented men and women. As the years passed, I became more philosophical about periods of unemployment. That doesn't mean they got any easier; it means we became more experienced in dealing with them.

Sixteen years ago, after moving into our third home, which was necessarily larger than our earlier homes, due to our larger family, I commented to my husband that we might be spreading ourselves too thin. We had a large house payment that we could barely afford if nothing unforeseen happened, such as a large repair bill, medical bill, or other unbudgeted expense. Everything unbudgeted happened, however. Also, within two months of buying our new house, we were unemployed.

The multi-national computer company my husband had been working for suddenly ran out of contracts, and tens of thousands of employees had to be cut worldwide. My husband was one of them. His unemployment lasted six months. Our close relatives and friends would say, "If you need anything, let us know." Need anything? At that time we had a family of five children who were in the habit of eating, plus we had huge house payments and other expenses that used up our meager savings, but there was no income.

After a couple months of shattered expectations and "almost got it" job prospects, my confidence was shattered. I remember sitting on my bed one morning, crying for all of us. I became so depressed I was questioning God about our bad luck. Why us, Lord? Then, remembering back to the birth of our first child, a boy, I recalled looking at him and praying for his health and safety. My prayer for him then, and the prayer for all our other children when they were born was, "Please Lord, don't let anything happen to the children. I realize we all have problems. If we can choose ours, let them be financial." (My resilient husband has reminded me long since, "Enough already!")

Suddenly a strange feeling overwhelmed me. As I sat on the bed crying, I began looking out the window. I saw a beautiful, unusual sight. Our neighbor's front hill across the street was covered with sparrows hopping about, cheerily pecking away at seeds and worms. As I watched them enjoying their feeding, the words, "How much more you, oh you of little faith," overwhelmed my body and mind. Immediately I went downstairs to tell my husband everything would be all right. We're in the hands of a loving God.

Children should be allowed to share family crises. They don't have to know every detail, but they should know something about

158

what's happening. Although children don't have the same crises as parents, they should at least be told what their parents are suffering through. It's important children know that their parents are dealing successfully with life's difficulties. Later, when bad things happen in the children's lives, they'll have the good example of their parents to guide them. Parents who shelter their children from hard times may be doing them a disservice. Caring and sharing parents should help their children realize that hard times will pass, just as they did for mom and dad.

51

Making Wise Judgments

As children and adults, we're constantly making judgments. If we have good judgment, we have the ability to form an opinion objectively and wisely. If we have bad judgment, we're still forming opinions, but unobjectively and unwisely. Each of us, every day of our lives, is forming opinions.

How do children learn to judge wisely? By being judged wisely. Parents should encourage their children to ask for help when needed. Also, children should be encouraged to get outside support when it's needed, so that any false assumptions or rash judging can be avoided. Children need to see parents setting the example of seeking help when situations get out of control.

When parents or their children have been maliciously wronged by someone, it's very difficult, for example, to turn the other cheek. They want revenge to be swift and complete. But revenge is a dead end street. Mothers used to say, "God will punish them." Children then thought those who wronged them would eventually burn in hell. What is later discovered, is that if left to a higher power, offensive persons will somehow get their punishment in this life, in full view of the offended persons. Some call this "poetic justice."

Believing in such justice can be comforting. It removes a great burden from our shoulders to know we don't have to come up with a difficult punishment for someone. It helps remove sorrow, hatred, remorse, or anger from our minds, so that we can replace these bad feelings with good feelings. When justice is left to the Lord, we don't have to bother with it ourselves.

By walking away from and forgetting a bad incident, a person minimizes its importance and limits its influence. For example, what do you do if your child is cheated, harassed, rejected, belittled, or cursed at school? Judgment in the form of revenge does seem sweet. However, revenge focuses two spotlights, one on the person who is seeking revenge, and one on the person who is the object of revenge. Neither exposure is positive. Teach your child to walk away from "no-win" situations, so your child's character can grow strong. Peace of mind and self-esteem can grow also. Then, if any persons are evil to your child again, your child will be able to rise above such evil, and the psychiatrist's couch will be cheated out of another patient.

52

Thoughts About Suicide

Suicide has almost become epidemic among young people today. Most of our eight children have known someone from their own school or a nearby school who committed suicide. What's hard to understand, is how can life become so desperate so early?

Many child suicides have been attributed to drugs and alcohol, which destroy good judgment, but what about suicides that aren't drug related? How are they explained?

Families and friends are devastated. Some never recover. How do we convince children that life isn't easy for anyone? Without suffering through the lows that come, people can't experience the highs that follow.

Parents should help their children understand that problems aren't experienced by just a few persons. Everyone has problems of one kind or another. It's the serious problems that seem insurmountable at first. Eventually, however, given some effort and maybe even some outside help, serious problems can be overcome. When they are, they're soon forgotten and life goes on as before, sometimes even better.

Maybe parents haven't shared the bad times with their children as much as they've shared the good. Maybe children think parents never have serious problems if parents don't share those problems with their children. For example, a father's sudden unemployment and eventual new job may teach children who face a similar situation years later, that such a serious problem is common, and merely temporary. Children need to understand that while parents have disappointments and failures in life, they also experience pleasant surprises and releases from life's burdens. Such sharing by parents of both bad and good times is important for developing a balanced outlook in children.

Children from wealthy suburbs sometimes can't cope with life away from home. They feel like failures in their now meager surroundings. Perhaps those children need to be told about the difficult early lives and marriage their parents survived. Then children will understand that *life gets better*, and that their parents eventually got through the tough times. Sometimes, looking back, the early years even seem the best, as memories of early problems fade, and thoughts about good times grow.

Maybe society is approaching life too carelessly. It seems we can't turn on TV, or read a newspaper or magazine, without hearing about abortion, adultery, murder, rape, suicide, violence, drugs, or alcoholism, whether in the news, a talk show, or some other program. Child abuse and incest are frequent media story plots, together with immoral sexual activity in a heterosexual or homosexual vein. Seems that anything goes. Kisses and other sexual activities become so prolonged and passionate they're an embarrassment to view. Media representatives say they're mirroring life. Questions parents should ask are whose life? Why? Does it promote the general welfare and common good of the viewing public?

Women are encouraged to decide whether they want to have children *after* their children have already been conceived rather than *before*. Children in the womb are no longer valued. Too often, when children are already born into this life, they're rejected as an unfortunate inconvenience. Child-rejecting feelings of some parents even continue into the teen years of their children, creating serious psychological problems in those children.

Society's values are getting confused and distorted. Maybe some child suicides involve children with high moral values, who just can't cope with the moral decadence that's represented to them on TV as reality. Maybe these children become so overwhelmed and depressed by society's moral decay, that suicide seems an acceptable escape.

Now, in a time of shockingly bad morality on TV and in movies, it's reassuring to see that at least a few of the good programs are winning awards. Also, a few movies that adhere to high moral standards are winning awards. For example, on TV, "The Bill Cosby Show" dared to entertain us with moral people striving to lead moral lives. It was voted the best. Some years ago, the movie *Gandhi* dared to deal with such themes as racial justice, self-discipline and non-violence. It was voted best.

All the media should dare to be great. The problem is, greatness takes time, teamwork, and talent; immorality can be portrayed quickly, easily, and shockingly by any idiot.

The bottom line is that parents can control the media. If they reject bad programs, those programs will eventually get cancelled. A protest letter to a sponsor carries great influence. For example, it takes only three letters to some sponsors to force a meeting of the board of directors.

People don't live the way some soaps and other TV programs or movies would have us believe. Parents shouldn't let their kids grow up thinking life is like the media represents it to be. Parents should help children realize life is good, even though it's not trouble-free. Life has its failures as well as successes, its share of the good as well as the bad. Life shows us the sun after the rain. Parents should teach their children to respect life as a blessing and gift from God, and that life should end only when God chooses, not when people choose.

53

Maintaining Respect

Parents can be defied by their children at any time. No matter when it happens, it's scary. At a very early age, one of my daughters defied me. She was between one and one-and-one-half years old, and in training pants. When this child got angry with me, she simply took off her pants and urinated on the carpet. Then she would stick around for awhile to see how shocked I would be. It was so long ago, I can't remember any details except cleaning the rug and being plenty upset. At this late date, I wonder why I didn't make her clean it up.

In contrast, one of my boys, a quiet, stubborn child, defied me in a different, but non-threatening way. He simply went up to the dresser in my room and rearranged all the various bottles of perfume, lipstick, make-up, and nail polish I kept on a glass tray. Then, just as quietly, he went back to his room. When I saw my tray rearranged, I knew I had done something to get his goat.

Relationships are a little different when children get older. If parents are always viewed as the boss, and the children are regarded as workers and servants, the parent-child relationship may be adversarial. To avoid this situation, parents should try to be fair at all times. That way, conflicts won't lead to confrontations and defiance.

A friend of mine, the mother of six teenagers, has a beautiful relationship with her children. Since most parents seem to have difficulty handling their teenagers, I asked my friend her secret for success. What makes her different from other parents? She told me it's her attitude. She doesn't treat her children as puppets who take orders from her and have no minds of their own. Rather, she respects the personality and individualism of each child, and they all meet on equal ground with equal respect. That's not to say she comes down to their level; rather, she raises them up to hers. Also, they're all good friends.

To be practical, what does a mother do if her child defies her? If she says, "Be home by 10:00," and the child says, "No!"; or if she grounds a child, and the child simply ignores the grounding; what does a mother do? She can scold and punish until she's worn out and frustrated. Or, she can kick the child out of the house, so that the child can live by his or her own rules. If the child is over 18, that may simply be the best solution available.

When parents are no longer respected by an older child, that respect usually is difficult to regain. Therefore, before it's too late, something should be done. The question is, what? The answer is, back to the basics; back to love, being with one's children, regarding children as individuals with unique talents and personalities, and loving them and respecting them for their individualism.

Much of how teenagers behave goes back to their childhood, and how much they respected their parents, or if their parents were even around to earn respect. Trouble usually doesn't develop overnight; it has been brewing for years.

It has been heard so much, but it bears repeating: parents should keep the lines of communication open. They don't have to ask all kinds of questions and pry into their children's affairs. Conversation

166

can be about anything at all. Parents should strive to talk *with* their children, rather than *at* them. As parents, we need to be *good listeners*. We must remember that a conversation consists of *two* people talking *together*. We should try to hear beyond their words what our children are saying.

Sometimes, in spite of everything parents do, nothing goes right. Their child is approaching the age when it's time to go to college or get a job and find an apartment. Quite often a most loving child can, as a young adult, begin giving parents some terrible times. After leaving home, however, kids seem to eventually shape up, unless they have a drug, alcohol, or other serious problem.

Keep in mind that the troublesome, disrespectful child may be the one who really loves home the most. Family is extremely important to children. A child's bad behavior may simply be a means of trying to reduce or compensate for the pain of leaving home. It might be that child's mental defense mechanism against sorrow. Whatever the reason, whether external or internal, a child's troublesome behavior can be frustrating to parents. Parents should console themselves with the thought that such troublesome behavior will pass, though sometimes it passes far too slowly. Fortunately, most situations have a happy ending, even though for a few years it seems that parents may have lost their children's respect.

54

Motivating The Stubborn Child

Ever notice how a stubborn child is often quiet as well? Almost from birth a child's stubbornness may be noticed by parents, but parents learn to deal with it through experience. For example, a parent should never be short with a stubborn child, or rush a question. In fact, if a task can be described to a stubborn child in an unhurried, non-threatening, and friendly way, a lot more can be accomplished. This approach is preferred for everyone, but it's imperative with a stubborn child.

"Take the garbage out right now!" will never get it done. "Johnny, could you please take the garbage out for me?" will usually get it done cheerfully.

"Be sure to cut the grass today!" doesn't get it done. A motivating alternative might be, "Johnny, the grass is getting really long. I'd appreciate it if you could cut it some time this week, when you can find the time to get it done."

It's *how* a parent asks a question that usually determines what gets done. A stubborn child needs rational explanations for a parent's requests. As in the grass-cutting request, parents not only need to ask the question non-threateningly, they also need to ask it slowly, and in a logical way. If parents can just ask for something in the form of a gracious question, their stubborn child is likely to respond with a much happier and more positive reply than the child who isn't stubborn.

At first, parents who give orders grow more frustrated, and so does the stubborn child. As parents get a good handle on the situation, however, a good relationship begins to grow. It's not reasonable to expect that Mom will *always* be able to take time, or even *feel* like taking time, to slowly and thoughtfully word a question for a stubborn child. Don't worry, nobody's expected to be perfect. It takes concentrated effort to word a question carefully and non-threateningly, but it pays big dividends. It's also a good habit to develop when dealing with all children. The peace it brings to the household is worth the effort.

55

Forgetting Disagreements; Keeping Promises

A bad memory doesn't disqualify people from parenthood; it sometimes makes it easier. Also, a parent's bad memory can frustrate children. Many times, however, it isn't so much bad memory as utter confusion.

Have you ever been in the situation where you're talking to one child, and another interrupts? Then, add another child, plus, add dad. You stop a sentence midway into your conversation with number one, get distracted into listening to number two, and so on, and on, and on. Now you come back to number one, but can't finish the interrupted sentence, because you can't remember what it was about. Maybe you think you're getting senile, or that you're losing your memory. Don't worry, the computer in your head was just overloaded.

A true memory lapse occurs when you become angry with a child, then an hour later can't remember the cause of your anger. Everyone picks up where the good times left off. That's as it should be. No troubles are so terrible they can't be cured. If troubles can't be remembered for even an hour, they're probably insignificant.

Parents need to remember, though, that troubles should be insignificant to everyone involved. If they aren't, a child may remember the bad experience, or what he feels was the unfairness of your feelings. In that situation you could end up dealing with a brooder. An unfortunate incident can continue to boil and brew until possibly many years later, it has to be uncovered in therapy in order to be released. If you're dealing with problems and have a short memory, be sure the problems are forgotten by everyone else as well. Poor remembrance of disagreements is often a blessing. Forgetting disagreements promotes harmony.

However, poor memory in keeping important promises and appointments is not a good thing. Parents need to be very careful about what they promise. Once a commitment is made to children, it's etched in stone. They'll never forget or let you forget, either. Better to write it down. Put it on a calendar. If you have any doubts about your availability, admit you don't know, and say that you'll know when you've checked for other commitments.

An interesting contrast to a parent's poor memory is that their children have excellent memories, especially of any commitments parents have made. For example, if a child gets grounded, and you give the dates of the grounding, the child will usually respect those dates, even if you yourself don't remember them. I recall such an incident involving my 14-year-old daughter. She was grounded for a weekend. When the weekend arrived, I couldn't believe I was seeing her at home and, having forgotten she was grounded, I wondered why. After the weekend was half over, I asked her what was going on. She said, "You forgot! You actually forgot I was grounded! I could have been out all weekend!" That's the way a bad memory can bounce. Win a few, lose a few.

VIII. Mothering Mothers

56

Ignoring "Mom, C'mere!"

Would you believe after more than 30 years of marriage kids are still saying, "Mom, c'mere" and I'm still going? Worse yet, I still "c'mere" when my husband says those two frustrating words. Am I nuts?

Only recently am I remembering to tell the children that they're younger than I am, so they'll have to come to me. I can be working in the kitchen and a child yells, "Mom, c'mere!" So I take my hands out of the dish water, dry them, rush out, and ask the body sprawled on the couch, "What do you want?"

I've become smarter in many ways over the earlier years of my life, but this isn't one of those times. I'm getting a little better with lines like, "You're younger than me, c'mere!" Or how do you like, "If you're calling me I can't hear because the water's running, c'mere!" Or maybe, "I've hurt my foot, you'll have to c'mere!"

175

Women must constantly be alert for opportunities to upgrade themselves from the servant class. We've suppressed ourselves for so many years, we oldsters have a hard time changing.

Can you imagine young women today answering to a "C'mere!"? Work should be getting more evenly distributed between husbands, wives, and children. Everyone has to pitch in and help. Maybe "Mom c'mere," which never made the dictionary, will also get thrown out of the home.

57

How To Make Volunteering Pay

A Volunteer is a person who performs some service willingly, without any requirement to do so. Or, volunteering is a process of offering oneself for some service at one's own discretion and often without compensation. That's how a dictionary might define "volunteer."

Another definition would add that, "Volunteers are moms." Of course fathers are volunteers as well, but usually moms outnumber them. Want to do a little tutoring at school? How about helping with a music or art enrichment program? How about working at a school carnival, sport exchange, teachers' luncheon, fine arts fair, book fair? Why not become a room mother or PTA president? How about volunteering for church work, welcoming newcomers, or planning a graduation party? Want to help hospitals, serve on a calling committee, or join the Community Resource Pool? The list of

177

volunteer opportunities is a long one, limited only by one's imagination.

There seems to be a natural growth to volunteering. Many home bound moms start volunteering for calling committees, then progress to bigger jobs as their time and talents permit. The natural opportunity that selfless volunteer moms forget to take advantage of, is the one that moves them beyond volunteering to actually cashing in on the wonderful knowledge and experience they've acquired. Many times when kids are in school, moms find the need to go beyond volunteering and earn enough money to supplement the family income, or help get their kids through college. But what can moms do? Where should they start?

Go to the principal of your school, the head of your church's women's club, the hospital, or any other place you've worked as a volunteer. Ask the persons you've worked so hard for to write you a letter of recommendation concerning those wonderful talents you've shared so generously with their organizations. Remember also that you've been a manager for many years, right in your own home. Believe in yourself, have self-confidence, develop a comprehensive resume, and others will soon recognize your talent. Also, add another word after the word "volunteer;" add "job," because that's what it's been for a number of years. As a volunteer, you have held an important job and were very much employed.

When you think of volunteering for any non-paying activity, keep in mind the kind of paying job that might interest you in the future. Then volunteer for something related to that paying job. Make volunteer work count for you personally as well as for your community. Use volunteer work to build up your job experience and fill out your resume.

Businessmen and government officials are starting to recognize that women with volunteer experience are excellent employees. A woman with volunteer experience does her work reliably and well, not because some boss is forcing her to, but because for years she has learned to work to the best of her abilities with no supervisor looking over her shoulder, and with no monetary reward whatsoever. The former volunteer is not only a trustworthy employee, she's cheerful, businesslike, budget-conscious, and uncomplaining. Now all that's left for businessmen or government officials to do is hire her at a fair wage and appreciate their good fortune that she agreed to accept the job.

58

You Know You've Volunteered Long Enough When...

...You're head of a school event and you haven't had any children in the school for the last two years.

...All the other committee members are young enough to be your children, and some are.

...You can do any job better than anyone else.

...You can't think up any more original decorations.

...All of the original women you began volunteering with are grandmothers and you're still volunteering in grade school.

...You've heard every speaker available on the circuit at least once.

...You've used all your salad recipes for luncheons.

...There are no open days left on your calendar because of all the committee meetings you attend.

...Your kids think you're the babysitter and your husband thinks you're his mistress.

...You do your housework regularly between 10:00 p.m. and 1:00 a.m.

...Yours is the first name to be mentioned to head any difficult project.

...You're becoming a saint because you lack enough leisure time to become a sinner.

...Your house is the pits, so you volunteer to avoid cleaning it.

...There's no more underwear left in your family's drawers, and they've already turned each pair inside out.

...You can't remember quickly how many children you have or how old they are.

...People you meet in the business world can't hold a candle to your organizational ability.

...You finally get time to call your best friend and find out she moved away three years ago.

...McDonalds comes to your house and builds "golden arches" over your front door, because you're their best customer.

59

Staging a Burn-Out

Burn-out affects almost every person at some time in life. Many women start experiencing it when kids are finishing grade school, or during high school years. It usually begins in the home. Mothers get sick of cleaning house, washing clothes, and preparing meals. They're tired of preparing creative meals that get gulped down in five to ten minutes, often while the eater is standing and talking on the telephone.

A mother keeps cleaning the house over and over, dusting the same furniture, scrubbing the same floors, washing the same bathrooms year after year. Then, suddenly, she discovers she's the parent of teenagers who become genetic throwbacks to the caveman era. Their rooms are pits. They hibernate in them, grunt to be fed, then return to lock the door, blast the stereo, and study(?). Litter permeates the house. Mother doesn't feel good about her cleaning anymore, because she knows she's in the same house with a volcano.

What the heck, if you can't beat 'em, join 'em. Let the glass tables have messages like "clean me" written all over them. Let dust balls grow to golf ball size, so they'll be useful.

Every morning you go down to the laundry room and find that nothing has changed; always three loads of wash. If you get sick and miss a day, six loads of wash. Wash, dry, fold. Can't let them wrinkle!

Become devious! Slip those wet towels from the shower directly into the dryer. Skip the wash machine. Why care? Who knows the difference? Go ahead, fold the sweater your teenager wore for only one hour, then slip it back to the kid unwashed. Return all the clothes the way they came to the wash. Shirts, socks, or t-shirts that are inside out, return them that way. Forget the wash for several days. Then when kids yell about their clothes, let them solve the problem themselves.

Forget the whole darn place. Go to lunch with your friends and commiserate with them. Go for a walk. Sit and read a book. Join a church committee. Break your work habits before they break you. Who says your house has to be cleaned on a certain day? Why are **you** the only one who cooks a meal, scrubs the toilets, or washes clothes? Revolt! Go on strike! Take time off! Go on a picnic!

Why do mothers keep themselves locked into schedules? When kids are young, schedules are important; but if there comes a burnout time, change is needed. Men switch jobs, kids have new and growing interests. Everyone changes. Why can't mom? Go for it! Change your routine! Whatever you do, don't look back at the dust balls!

60

Getting Away From It All

There comes a time when parents need a break from their kids. It could be that point in a marriage when husband and wife haven't had a meaningful conversation for over six months. Or maybe the sight of each other has become depressing rather than exciting. Wouldn't it be nice if parents could get away for a short vacation to one of the many attractive places in the United States?

Too expensive? Many local hotels have special weekend deals to tempt you. The problem is that if you don't go far enough away from home, your kids pop in to use the hotel pool, or maybe they phone you five times a day.

What's really a treat, is slipping off about 100 or so miles from home to a city with some charm to it. You want to get far enough away so you can't rush home for every imagined emergency, but you want to be close enough so you don't have to take out another mortgage on the house to pay for the trip.

I'm writing this right now in Duluth, Minnesota, 160 miles from our home. Our excuse was a cousin's college graduation combined with some business. It's not our first time here. Duluth grows on a person. Picture San Francisco, then divide it by 50 and you have Duluth.

This is a four-day trip for us. We left in the middle of May, the busiest month of the school year. We were so mentally drained and exhausted, we nearly cancelled out. Now, after two days, we're relaxed, rested, and refreshed. With all this new-found energy we might have to go home and join another committee. Imagine nothing better to do for four days than eat, sleep, shop, walk, sight-see, and, in general, pamper yourself with leisure time and relaxation. Some people like to go on religious retreats. This is another means of getting away. If it revitalizes marriage and family life, it's the thing to do.

The bottom line is time...time for you and your mate to speak to each other without interruptions, to be together without the telephone ringing; time to enjoy a splendid, leisurely meal that someone has not only prepared for you, but has also served you, so you don't have to clear the table, wash the dishes, or clean the kitchen; time to get up in the morning and leave the room in a mess, knowing that some efficient hotel or motel employee will have it orderly and cleaned when you return. The extra bonus comes when you return home to find out you were missed. It's great to get away!

61

Remembering Thoughtfulness

This story is about a thoughtful kindness over 20 years ago that will never be forgotten. Over the years, our lives change in many subtle, often drastic ways. We keep evolving and developing for bad or good. Our horizons become so expanded, that when we look back over past years, we see that we've progressed in many ways.

Thirty years ago there weren't as many two-income families. Either a wife worked while her husband completed college, or the husband worked while his wife stayed home and took care of their young children. Our situation was that my husband's military service, education, and postgraduate work occupied the first ten years of our marriage.

While my husband was working part-time on his doctorate program in Michigan, we had our first two children. After the birth of our first child, however, I no longer worked outside the home.

Instead, my husband began a full-time teaching job that turned out to be a financial disaster.

After our house payment, we had only $55 a week left for food, utilities, doctors, dentist, clothing, repairs, tuition, insurance, car payments and numerous other expenses. The result was that we were always broke and in debt.

One day, while I was carrying our second child, a neighbor volunteered to take me to my doctor appointment. On the way home she asked me if I'd like to stop for a donut and a cup of coffee. I didn't want her to know I was penniless, but my hesitation caused her to say, "I insist! It's my treat!" So we stopped, and she treated me to the most thoughtful, loving, considerate treat I have ever had in my life. I couldn't stop talking about it all night to my husband, and I also couldn't get over what rich neighbors we had!

We all need treats. Maybe it's helping a harried mom get away for an hour to go walking, visiting a shut-in, talking on the phone to a friend who needs a morale boost, having a close friend to share our hearts with (and that *doesn't* mean a spouse), or treating a broke and tired young mother to a simple donut and a cup of coffee. We have no way of knowing when a kindness we do for others may reappear. Maybe we're about to be impatient with our child, when a kind act someone did for us is suddenly remembered and prevents our impatience.

There are unusual events in each of our lives, but the memorable ones are sometimes so humble that we wonder why we remember them so well after so many years.

Whenever I see a donut now, I remember the day over 20 years ago when my dear, thoughtful neighbor treated me. Then I secretly wish her well and bless her in my heart.

62

Enjoying Family Gatherings

Family gatherings can be well planned, spontaneous, gourmet, or fast food. What's important is that the family is being reunited. At a time when geographical distances and other factors separate families, gatherings are becoming harder to arrange. Even holidays are pulling family members in so many different directions, it's hard getting them together again.

It's great hearing kids talking together at family gatherings to find out what's going on and what went on. Kids love to reminisce about what they got away with over the years. To hear them talk, it's plenty! Some things are cute, some maddening, some dangerous. Kids usually include moms in these sessions, because their big thrill is seeing if they can shock her.

"Remember how we used to say we were going to the library? We went shopping."

"Remember when we said Mary's mom was home so we could play in her house? She never was home."

"Remember how you thought I stayed in when I was grounded? I climbed out the window and snuck back home the same way."

There are probably worse episodes they describe when mom's gone. At our age, we'd probably have a heart attack if they confessed everything. It's fortunate that they spare us!

What's important is the presence of family members gathered together to assure each other support and love. If school or a job isn't going well, if life is a temporary upper or downer, the family cares. If one family member is on the outs, through whomever's fault, that member should be welcomed back to the family circle. Healing, feeding, fostering, loving, are gifts of the gathered family. If members of the same family can't love each other, how can they expect strangers to love them and wish them well?

It's not always easy to love those closest to us. How much easier to feed the hungry at a mission, visit the hospitalized, dance with the retarded, or give to a charity. Those are the easy things. It can often be harder to get along with members of our own families. That's the real test.

How polite we can be to friends and strangers, but what are we like to our own families? Are we polite to family members the way we are to strangers? Do we give of ourselves freely with no strings attached, the way we do when we give food, clothes, or services in charity to strangers? Do we talk to our own children in the same unhurried way we gossip with friends? Even co-workers of ours get more respect sometimes than we give our own children. Why does too much familiarity so often breed contempt? These are questions we need to answer.

Our families are not whipping posts for our problems of the day. They are, children and spouses alike, precious gifts to love, nourish, and cherish. A family gathering is where we should find loving, nourishing, and cherishing.

63

Making Sure House Rules Win

House rules aren't a big problem for little children. Children love direction and living by rules. Rules give them a sense of security. In fact, if young children were asked to select leniency or rules, they would be in favor of rules.

Teenagers do a turnaround. They fight rules just because they are rules. Through all the grumbling, however, teenagers secretly prefer direction. You just can't catch them admitting it or asking for it.

House rules get the true test when young adults go away to college, then return each summer; or when young working adults continue to live at home for awhile after their high school graduation. Parents will experience conflict in most cases. The ideal would be for parents to sit down with their young adults and review the house rules. Which ones still apply? Are there younger children to be considered?

It's often difficult for both parents and young adults living at home to decide which house rules stay, and which change or expand with adulthood. A little independence away from home can create problems when a young adult moves back home again. Late hours, for example, create a problem. Failure to help with household chores creates a problem, especially when younger children become resentful of the freeloader. It doesn't do a lick of good to broadcast it, but parents should remember, it's their house, and they're the boss.

If young adults and parents can't seem to get together on rules, it might be time for young adults to move out. No disgrace to that. Parents and children will keep their love for each other alive much longer when they're apart than when they're together sniping at each other.

The world has made it difficult for young people to become independent. Costs of everything have soared, often forcing families to remain together too long. Parents should be loving, patient, and understanding, but they needn't be a floor mat!

64

Why Women Need Women

A woman's best friends are other women. Family is wonderful, husbands are wonderful, but every woman needs other women. Family members sharing a difficult experience with mom aren't usually the best people to talk to for encouragement or advice. A woman needs other women who have already experienced what she's now going through, and who can help her in objective and supporting ways.

Kids will be kids, and, oh yes, husbands will be husbands. Most women experience the same frustrations with each. How can a mother survive? By finding out that her troubles aren't unique.

At times, a mother feels she's everybody's servant. She feels she has no other identity. Her husband may be a bit insensitive, self-centered, autocratic. She's not alone! She may even feel like chucking it all, as almost every woman occasionally feels like doing.

192

Women need to share such feelings with each other. They're each other's safety valves.

All this doesn't mean they're going to leave husband and children. It does mean that marriages might have a better chance of surviving if women could talk to women and be comforted, encouraged, reassured, and otherwise helped.

Now that more mothers are working at jobs outside the home, they aren't able to get together socially as often as before. It wouldn't be surprising if this fact contributed to the higher divorce rate. A safety-valve is bypassed, and since the steam has nowhere to go, it blows up the marriage.

Many women have helped save a few marriages, healed a few wounds, or encouraged each other to laugh at their problems. They've generally been good friends with each other. Women talk seriously to each other, and they speak with a sense of humor. They teach each other how to laugh, as they realize that there are no unique problems. In fact, the more women visit with each other, the more they realize just how common their situations are. Adjusting to marriage, having a family, raising children, doing housework, working at school, and helping at church and elsewhere, are some activities women have in common and can discuss with each other. What's important to women isn't always interesting to their families. That's why women need to talk with other women from their own peer group.

Men's needs seem different than women's, because men rarely admit to their deeper concerns. They seek companionship for bowling, lunch, hunting, softball or fishing. They don't usually admit needing the same kind of supportive relationship from men that women need from other women.

65

Suffering From Empty Nest Syndrome

Three words, "empty nest syndrome," are said to cause cold sweats and a feeling of desperation in all mothers. After a life of raising children, when the last one leaves, mothers all over the world are supposed to die of loneliness and boredom. They'll have nowhere to turn, no place to go, no people to visit, no desire to live.

Two years ago, after 2 1/2 children had moved out (one comes home from college each summer), I started worrying about the empty nest syndrome. During the school year, with only five children living at home, strange feelings began to overcome me. Feelings like, If I'm supposed to be feeling anxious, why am I so relaxed?

Am I supposed to be lonesome?

Why am I enjoying my leisure so much?

Why is life so satisfying?

Free Time! Blessed free time.

Joy!

And on and on, relief and joy.

What in the world is the matter with me, I thought? I love my children, why aren't I desolate? All the articles I had read about the approaching empty nest syndrome said I would be fretting about what was in store for me. However, my children are only beginning to leave home. Maybe I should question my friends and acquaintances who are now alone, who have no children living at home anymore. After asking these mothers what feelings they have, now that all their children are gone, I discovered that sentiments are the same. A pattern quickly becomes evident. These mothers are all "suffering" with *unmitigated joy!*

My question was the same for all of them, "The Empty Nest Syndrome, tell me what it's like." Without exception, the answer was, "WONDERFUL!" There were no long faces, no sadness, no regrets. Only one thing that marred their joy; kids moving back home once they had left!

Order extra copies for relatives and friends. Please send
_____copy (s) of *Surviving Motherhood* to:

Your Name:_____

Address:_____

City/State/Zip:_____

Enclosed find $_____for _____copy(s).
Price List: $6.95 U.S./$7.95 Canada
Add $1.50 mailing cost for each book ordered.
Mail order to: St. John's Publishing
                  6824 Oaklawn Avenue
                  Edina, MN 55435

Order extra copies for relatives and friends. Please send
_____copy (s) of *Surviving Motherhood* to:

Your Name:_____

Address:_____

City/State/Zip:_____

Enclosed find $_____for _____copy(s).
Price List: $6.95 U.S./$7.95 Canada
Add $1.50 mailing cost for each book ordered.
Mail order to: St. John's Publishing
                  6824 Oaklawn Avenue
                  Edina, MN 55435
